From Your Friends At **The MAILBOX®**

JULY

A MONTH OF IDEAS AT YOUR FINGERTIPS!

PRESCHOOL– KINDERGARTEN

WRITTEN BY
Barbara Backer, Diane Gilliam, Linda Gordetsky, Ada Goren,
Lucia Kemp Henry, Lori Kent, Angie Kutzer, Suzanne Moore, Sharon Murphy,
Vicki Mockaitis Pacchetti, Mackie Rhodes, Dayle Timmons, Virginia Zeletzki

EDITED BY
Lynn Bemer Coble, Jayne M. Gammons, Ada Goren, Laurel Robinson,
Jennifer Rudisill, Debbie Shoffner, Gina Sutphin

ILLUSTRATED BY
Jennifer Bennett, Cathy Spangler Bruce, Pam Crane, Clevell Harris,
Lucia Kemp Henry, Susan Hodnett, Sheila Krill, Mary Lester, Rob Mayworth,
Kimberly Richard, Rebecca Saunders, Barry Slate, Donna K. Teal

TYPESET BY
Scott Lyons, Lynette Maxwell

COVER DESIGNED BY
Jennifer Bennett

www.themailbox.com

Manufactured in the United States

10 9 8 7 6 5 4 3

TABLE OF CONTENTS

July Calendar

National July-Belongs-To-Blueberries Month

Summertime is blueberry time! And July happens to be the peak month for fresh blueberries. Celebrate this tasty berry by making a pan of Blueberry Bliss with your students' help. A serving of this sweet treat is extra yummy with a scoop of ice cream or a dollop of whipped topping on top!

Blueberry Bliss

(makes 24 half-cup servings)

20-ounce can crushed pineapple, undrained
1 package yellow cake mix
3 cups fresh blueberries
1/2 cup sugar
1/2 cup melted butter or margarine
1 cup chopped pecans (optional)

Lightly butter a 9" x 13" cake pan. Spread the pineapple on the bottom of the pan; then sprinkle on the cake mix, the blueberries, and the sugar. Drizzle the melted butter over the top and add the nuts, if desired. Bake at 350° for 45 minutes or until bubbly.

National Recreation And Parks Month

This monthlong observance highlights leisure activities for young and old alike. Mark this special month by asking youngsters to share their favorite recreational activities. What do they like to do best when they visit a local park? Roller-skate? Picnic? Enjoy the playground equipment? If possible take a field trip to a local park and encourage them to participate in some favorite pastimes. Take photos while you're there; after developing the photos, post them on a bulletin board titled "Park It!"

Jimmy likes mustard on a hot dog.

National Hot Dog Month

Did you know that Americans eat more than 16 billion hot dogs a year? Have some fun with this all-American food favorite by creating a class book. To prepare cut simple hot-dog and bun shapes from tagboard. Invite each child to trace around a hot-dog shape on red construction paper and around a bun shape on tan construction paper. Have him cut out his hot dog and bun, then glue them onto white drawing paper as shown. Direct him to use crayons to add the toppings of his choice. On each child's paper, write his dictated completion to this sentence: "[Child's name] likes [toppings] on a hot dog." Bind the pages between construction-paper covers and add the title "Hungry For Hot Dogs."

Space Week (week including July 20)

On July 20, 1969, astronauts Neil Armstrong and Edwin "Buzz" Aldrin first landed on the moon. A number of states commemorate this important date in history with a weeklong celebration of human explorations into space. Mark the anniversary of the moon landing by sharing Eric Carle's *Papa, Please Get The Moon For Me* (Simon & Schuster Books For Young Readers). After reading the story, talk with your students about the real phases of the moon that led to this fictional story. Then provide a variety of silver art materials (such as silver crayons, aluminum foil, rickrack, or silver glitter), glue, and white drawing paper cut into circles and crescents. Invite each child to choose a moon shape and decorate it with the sparkling silver materials. Hang the finished projects from your classroom ceiling as shiny reminders of Space Week.

4—Independence Day

The Fourth of July is the birthday of the United States. What better way to celebrate than with a birthday cake? In advance prepare an unfrosted sheet cake from your favorite packaged mix. Purchase canned white frosting and some decorator icing in red and blue, as well as some red, white, and blue birthday candles. Invite youngsters to take turns helping you decorate the cake with squiggles, stripes, stars, or whatever they like. Add some candles (light them if fire codes permit) and sing a rousing rendition of "Happy Birthday To You" before slicing and serving the cake. (Find more ideas for celebrating this patriotic holiday in the unit on pages 6–15.)

8—Birthday Of Raffi

Raffi Cavoukian has brought musical joy and learning to millions of young children. He was born on this date in 1948 in Cairo, Egypt. If Raffi is a classroom favorite of your students, celebrate his special day by planning several "Raffi Breaks" throughout the day. In advance gather some Raffi recordings—such as *Singable Songs For The Very Young, Rise And Shine,* or *Bananaphone* (all produced by Troubadour Records Ltd.). Throughout the day, pause between activities to play a Raffi song or two and encourage little ones to sing along or to act out the lyrics.

10—Don't Step On A Bee Day

Summer means warm weather and thick grass just perfect for bare feet. But this day serves as a reminder to "bee" careful out there! Emphasize the importance of barefoot safety with this activity that sharpens gross-motor skills, too. Begin by using masking tape to outline a hopscotch grid on a carpeted area of your classroom. Prepare a simple bee cutout and laminate it for durability if desired. Randomly place the bee on a square of the grid. Then encourage each child to take a turn hopscotching barefoot. Caution her not to hop in the square with the bee. Then buzz the bee cutout to a different square for the next player.

Hey, watch out!

24—Cousins Day

Some of your students may be very familiar with their cousins. Others may not have any cousins, or their cousins may live far away. Familiarize little ones with the family relationships that produce cousins by drawing a simple diagram on your chalkboard (perhaps showing some of your own cousins). Draw the diagram again on a sheet of paper, add a quick note instructing parents to draw a similar diagram that names their child's cousins, and copy it for each child to take home. Have the children return the diagrams; then make a graph to compare the number of cousins each child has. Allow time for children who want to tell about their cousins to share their stories.

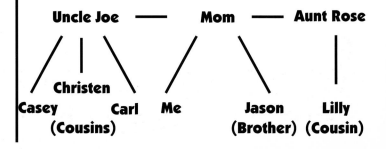

4

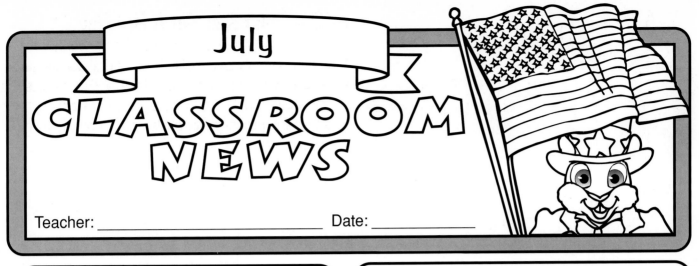

July

CLASSROOM NEWS

Teacher: _____   Date: _____

A Peek At The Week

Looking Ahead

Reminders

Help Wanted

Special Thanks

Hooray For The Red, White, And Blue!

Introduce your little ones to the idea of patriotism with this star-spangled unit. Try these ideas for the Fourth of July, or for any patriotic holiday during the year.

ideas contributed by Lucia Kemp Henry

Everything's Coming Up Red, White, And Blue

Get youngsters in the spirit by decorating your classroom with a patriotic flair! Hang lots of red, white, and blue crepe-paper streamers and American flags on your walls or from your ceiling. Gather pictures of famous places in the USA—such as the White House, the Lincoln Memorial, or Mount Rushmore—and add these to the decor. Cut a class supply of construction-paper stars in red, white, and blue, and label each one with a child's name. Attach the star cutouts to children's seats or cubbies. When your classroom is an all-American dream, invite little ones to begin your patriotic study by singing the song at right.

The Red, White, And Blue
(sung to the tune of "Happy Birthday To You")

Oh, the red, white, and blue.
Oh, the red, white, and blue.
Give a cheer we can all hear
For the red, white, and blue!
(Cheer loudly.)

Oh, the red, white, and blue.
Oh, the red, white, and blue.
Stand up tall and give your all
For the red, white, and blue!
(Stand tall and salute.)

Oh, the red, white, and blue.
Oh, the red, white, and blue.
Shout hooray every day-ay
For the red, white, and blue!
(Shout, "Hooray!")

Free-Form Flags

Invite youngsters to add to the red, white, and blue decor by making these free-form flags. Have each child select a 12" x 18" sheet of red, white, or blue construction paper to use as a background. Then set out paper scraps in red, white, and blue; scissors; glue; and gummed foil stars or precut paper stars. Encourage each child to cut shapes from the paper scraps and glue them onto his banner background to create an original flag design. Have him add stars to complete his banner. Display the finished flags on your classroom walls or on a bulletin board, or hang them from a length of fishing wire or yarn strung between two classroom walls.

My Own Old Glory

After little ones make their own creative designs with the project described in "Free-Form Flags," encourage them to attempt more specific replicas of the U.S. flag. Begin by displaying an American flag and giving youngsters a brief lesson on the reasoning behind its design, including the 13 stripes that represent the 13 original colonies, and the 50 stars that represent the 50 states. Then provide each child with a 12" x 18" sheet of white construction paper and a 6" x 9" piece of blue construction paper. Demonstrate how to glue the blue rectangle in the upper left-hand corner of the white sheet. Then provide gummed foil stars and invite each child to affix as many as she desires to her blue rectangle. Set out red tempera paint and wide paintbrushes, and have each child finish her own Old Glory by painting red stripes across the remaining white background.

If desired, set the finished flags aside for use with the "Patriotic Parade" activity on page 11.

Tri-Colored Treats

After the flag making, invite your little ones to enjoy some red, white, and blue treats. Serve vanilla ice cream with strawberry topping and blue-tinted whipped cream, or a simple fruit salad of sliced strawberries, blueberries, and banana wheels. Be sure to put these treats in clear plastic cups to show off their colors. Now those are treats fit for a…president!

Our Country

Of course, the USA means more than red, white, and blue and the Stars and Stripes. Engage your students in an age-appropriate discussion about our country. Jump-start the conversation by pointing out the pictures of famous American places on display in your classroom and showing a map of the United States. More advanced students will enjoy the beautiful artwork in the book *America The Beautiful* illustrated by Neil Waldman (Atheneum). While preschoolers and kindergartners may be too young to fully appreciate the freedoms we enjoy as Americans, they'll certainly appreciate the beauty of our great land.

Simple Songs

Many traditional patriotic songs involve difficult lyrics and abstract concepts. Teach your youngsters these very simple songs accompanied by familiar tunes.

It's My USA!
(sung to the tune of "BINGO")

My country is the USA—
The country that **I** love-o!
It's **my** USA.
It's **my** USA.
It's **my** USA.
The country that **I** love-o!

Sing the song two more times, replacing the boldfaced words with your *and* you *on the first repetition, and* our *and* we *on the last repetition.*

America Is Home
(sung to the tune of "Mary Had A Little Lamb")

America is big and wide, big and wide, big and wide!
America is big and wide, and it is home for me!

America is proud and free, proud and free, proud and free!
America is proud and free, and it is home for me!

America is you and me, you and me, you and me!
America is you and me, and it is home for me!

Patriotic Puzzles

Emphasize the shape of our nation with some made-in-the-USA puzzles. Locate a simple map of America and make several color copies. Glue the copies to tagboard; then cut around each map outline. Cut each map into three or four pieces for very young children, more for older students. Assign a different symbol (a shape, a number, or a letter) to each puzzle and label the back of each individual piece with that symbol to avoid mix-ups. Put each puzzle in a separate zippered plastic bag. Place all the puzzles in a center near your classroom map of the USA. Then invite little ones to work some map magic!

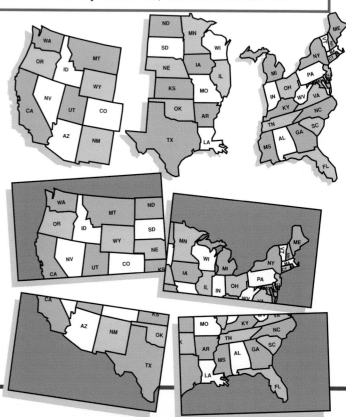

"All About America" Booklet

Encourage students to put together these booklets to help them become familiar with some American symbols. To prepare, duplicate a class supply of the booklet on pages 12–15 on white construction paper. Then read through the directions below, choose the method you'd like your students to use for each illustration, and gather the necessary materials. Have students work in small groups to complete their booklets, or invite the whole group to complete one page at a time. Discuss the booklet text as students work on each page. When all her pages are complete, have each child cut out her cover and pages, stack them in order, and staple her booklet along the left side. Then ask your patriotic preschoolers or kindergartners to take their booklets home to share with their families.

Cover: Write your name on the line. Color the rectangle in the top left corner with blue crayon. Draw red stripes across the rest of the flag. Stick some gummed foil stars or star-shaped stickers on the blue part of the flag.

The eagle is a symbol for America.

Page 1: Color the eagle brown with a white head and yellow beak and feet. Cut out the wing shapes and glue them onto the eagle as indicated. Or glue small craft feathers within the wing outlines.

Page 2: Color Uncle Sam. Place a real penny under the paper, beneath the circle on the left. Use a brown crayon to make a rubbing of the coin. Use a silver crayon to make a rubbing of a quarter in the middle circle and a nickel in the last circle. Or color the coin drawings at the top of the page, cut them out, and glue them in place on the page.

Page 3: Cut out the center section of the White House along the dotted lines. Glue it in place on the page. Color the sky blue and the grass green. Draw some trees on the White House lawn.

Everyone Loves A Parade!

Parades are a fun way for people to celebrate patriotic holidays such as the Fourth of July. Prepare your little ones to participate in some marching mania with the activities on these two pages.

Picture Books On Parade

Some of your youngsters may have never seen a real parade or may not remember their previous experiences. Share one or more of the following titles to get them in the marching mood!

Parade
Written by Donald Crews
Published by Greenwillow Books

Fourth Of July Bear
Written by Kathryn Lasky
Published by Morrow Junior Books

Thump, Thump, Rat-A-Tat-Tat
Written by Gene Baer
Published by HarperCollins
   Children's Books

Higgledy Piggledy Hobbledy Hoy
Written by Dorothy Butler
Published by Greenwillow Books

A Marching Poem

This bouncy chant will inspire youngsters to march their hearts out! Have your students form a circle and perform the movements as indicated.

March, march! We can march! We can march around.
(March in a circle.)
March, march! We can march! Stomping on the ground.
(March in place and stomp feet.)

March, march! We can march! March and hold my hand.
(Hold hands and march in place.)
March, march! We can march! Pretend that we're a band.
(March in place and pretend to play instruments.)

March, march! We can march! We can march as one.
(March in a circle with hands on neighbor's shoulders.)
March, march! We can march! Marching is such fun!
(March in circle and swing arms.)

Parade Preparations

Get your youngsters ready to perform in a parade of their own (see "Patriotic Parade") by helping them create appropriate red, white, and blue attire and some patriotic percussion instruments to accompany their marvelous marching!

Star-Spangled Shirts

In advance ask each family to send in a solid red, white, or blue T-shirt for their child. Purchase red, white, and blue fabric paints at your local craft store and gather a few sheets of cardboard. Cut several kitchen sponges into star shapes. Then, working with one or two children at a time, place a sheet of cardboard inside each child's T-shirt and lay it flat on a tabletop. Have each child dip the star sponges into shallow pans of fabric paint and print stars on his shirt. If desired, add some sparkle by sprinkling clear glitter over the wet paint. Allow the shirts to dry thoroughly (at least a day or two) before children wear them.

Happening Headbands

Provide each child with a red or blue construction-paper headband and a few star shapes cut from white construction paper. Have each youngster glue the stars onto her headband; then staple the band to fit her head.

Nifty Noisemakers

Give each child a 9" x 11" piece of white paper. Provide red and blue paint pens, glitter pens, or markers and have little ones decorate their papers. When the artwork is dry, assist each child in wrapping the decorated paper around an empty potato-chip can with a lid. Secure the paper with red or blue book tape or masking tape. Then place a handful of dried beans inside each can and replace the lid. Shake 'em up!

Patriotic Parade

End your celebration of the USA with a burst of color and fun! Ask parents if they can lend some tricycles and wagons to add to those you may already have at your school or center. Have youngsters help you decorate all the "parade vehicles" with red, white, and blue crepe-paper streamers. Then ask them to don their "Star-Spangled Shirts" and "Happening Headbands," grab their "Nifty Noisemakers" or the flags made in "My Own Old Glory" on page 7, and form a parade line. Bring along a portable cassette tape player and play a tape of marching music. Youngsters can take turns riding the trikes or pulling the wagons as you lead the parade around your school's hallways or grounds. Be sure to invite parents to attend this special event!

If desired, invite your students and their parents back to your classroom after the parade to enjoy some "Tri-Colored Treats" (see page 7). What a perfect way to note a patriotic day!

All About
America

by _____

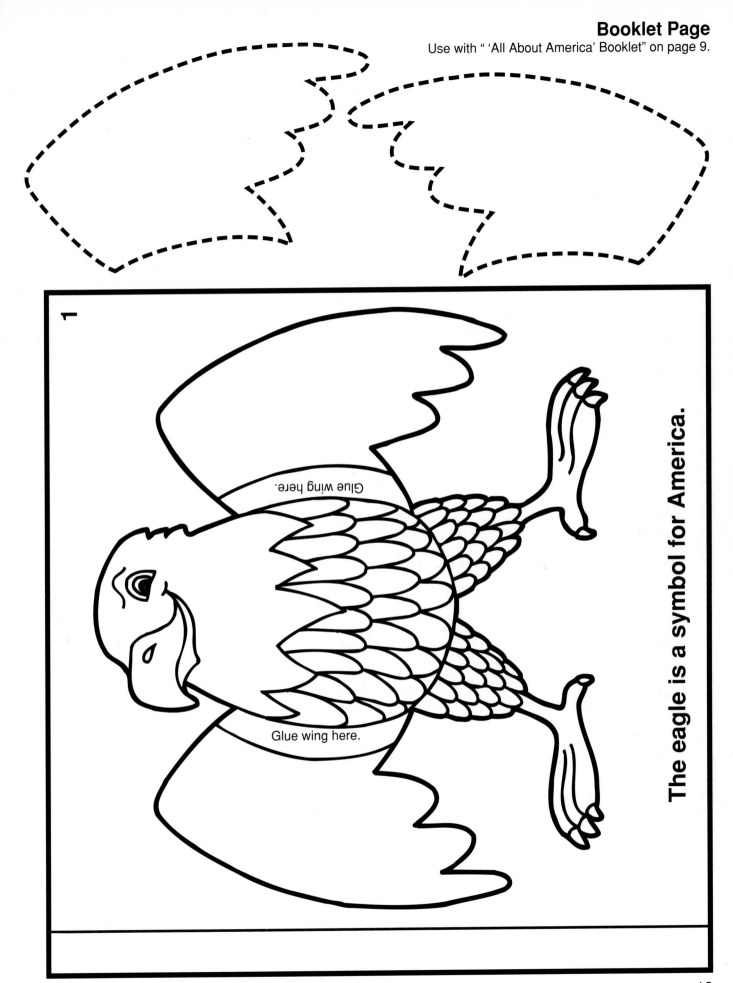

1

Glue wing here.

Glue wing here.

The eagle is a symbol for America.

13

penny

nickel

quarter

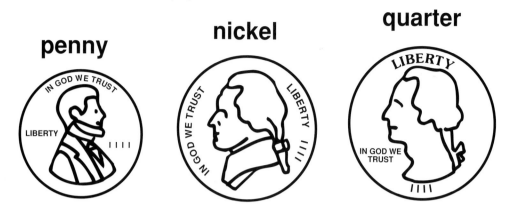

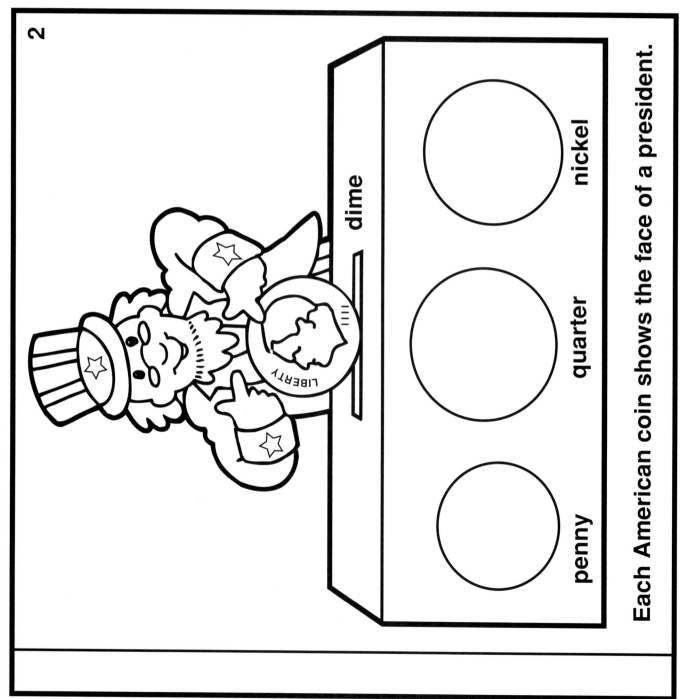

2

dime

nickel

quarter

penny

Each American coin shows the face of a president.

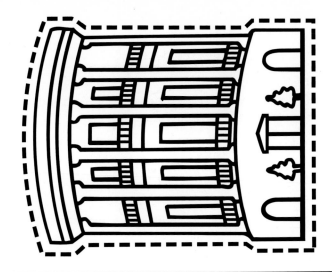

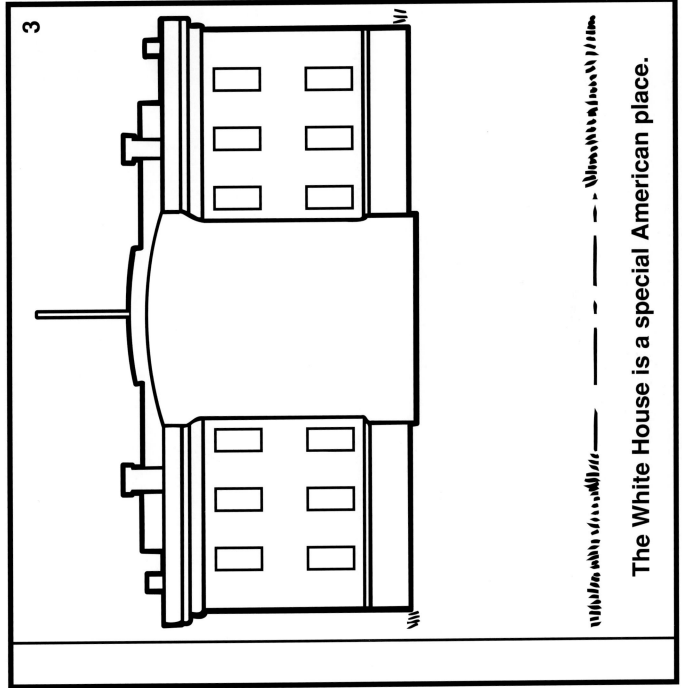

3

The White House is a special American place.

Getting Wet!

The heat is on! And there's no better way to cool down on a hot summer day than to get wet—whether from a light misting or from a soaked-to-the-bone drenching. Here's a deluge of ideas to choose from for a water-day celebration or just for a few beat-the-heat activities. Prior to your wet activities, send each child home with a copy of the letter on page 25 so that parents can plan and prepare ahead, too. Got your swimsuit and towel? Ready…set…let's get wet!

ideas contributed by Mackie Rhodes and dayle timmons

Bath-Time Blitz

Splish, splash! Let's all take a bath! Try this activity for some good, clean fun. Partially fill several wading pools (or large plastic tubs) with water; then add scented children's bubble bath to each pool. Finish filling the pools with a spray of water to create lots of foamy bubbles. Position the water hose or a sprinkler near the pools. Put several washcloths and a few water and bath toys in each pool; then add one or two seated children to each bubbly pool. Invite students to splash around, playing with the toys and taking an imaginary bath. If desired, inspire youngsters' bath-time "scrubbies" with a recording of Hap Palmer's "Take A Bath" from *Learning Basic Skills Through Music: Health And Safety* (Educational Activities, Inc.). After each child finishes his bath, encourage him to rinse off in a spray of water or under the sprinkler.

Shower Savvy

Do some of your youngsters prefer a shower to a bath? To accommodate these students, secure a hose with a sprayer attachment over a low-hanging tree branch or a piece of playground equipment. Supply the shower area with a washcloth, back scrubber, and shower cap; then turn on the water and lock the sprayer attachment so that a steady spray of water flows from it. Invite students to step into the shower, in turn, for a thoroughly delightful scrubbing. Don't be surprised to hear your shower-savvy students bellow a few operatic refrains above the pitter-patter of the water!

I'm singin' in the rain

Bathe The Babies

Students will immerse themselves in the roles of parenthood when they engage in this dramatic water-play activity. To begin, partially fill several plastic tubs with water to represent bathtubs. Add bubble bath, washcloths, sponges, and water-filled shampoo bottles to each of the tubs. Have towels, empty containers of baby powder, and powder puffs nearby. Invite each child, in turn, to bathe a plastic, immersible doll—her imaginary baby—in a tub. Encourage her to pamper her baby during bath time and afterwards with a gentle towel drying and powdering. If desired, prompt youngsters to sing a bath-time version of "This Is The Way" (sung to the tune of "Mulberry Bush").

Laundry Time

While youngsters are assuming the roles of parents, invite them to add their own flair to a redundant parental task—the laundry. To prepare, partially fill a water table or several plastic dishpans with water. Add a small portion of mild laundry detergent or a scented liquid soap to the water. To the side, set up a clothesline and a container of spring-type clothespins. Then have small groups of students take turns washing doll and baby clothes in the soapy water. Show them how to wring the water out of the washed items, then hang the clothes on the line to dry. With youthful enthusiasm and creativity, students will discover that grown-up chores can be fun!

A Wet Letter Day

Instead of a Wet T-shirt Day, why not have a Wet Letter Day—and accomplish a bit of classroom cleaning in the process? To begin, explain to your class that things in the classroom—like things in their homes—need to be cleaned periodically. Then select a letter of the alphabet, such as *T,* or any letter currently being studied. Have youngsters gather a collection of classroom items beginning with that letter that can be put in the water. For example, they might choose a towel, a T-shirt, a corresponding sponge letter, or plastic toys, such as a truck, a tiger, or a sand mold of the numeral 2. Ask each child to place her choice in a partially filled water table; then invite students to rotate turns playing at the water table. As youngsters engage in their wet letter play, encourage them to sound out the names of the items in the water, paying particular attention to the beginning sound of each. It's a Wet Letter Day!

17

At The Car Wash

Zoom on into this car wash to give youngsters a sudsy experience in categorizing and sequencing. In advance, ask each child to bring a plastic toy vehicle to class (or have him choose one from the classroom). After the collection of vehicles is gathered, set up an outdoor car-washing center. Equip the area with a hose with a sprayer attachment, a few water-filled spray bottles, small sponges, several tubs of soapy water, and a supply of dry washcloths or paper towels.

Then invite pairs of students to categorize the vehicles by color, size, or type. Ask the children to sequence the vehicles in a logical order before washing them. For example, the students might sequence all the red vehicles from smallest to largest. Or they might position all the cars to create a color pattern, or pattern the large vehicles according to type—such as *truck, car, car, truck.* After youngsters organize the vehicles, invite them to set about their car-wash work. If desired—and with the appropriate permission granted—you might even have youngsters wash a *real* car. Spray, scrub, rinse, dry. Zoom!

We Do Windows!

If you want to score points with your school's janitorial staff, this idea is clearly for you. In advance, secure permission from your principal or director to have your students clean the school's windows. Then ask a janitorial representative to visit your class. During her visit, tell youngsters that they are going to help her and her staff clean the school's windows. Ask your visitor to demonstrate proper window-cleaning techniques to the class, using child-safe supplies and equipment. If desired, invite each child to take a trial turn at cleaning a window in your classroom. Afterward take your class and the necessary supplies around the school to clean the accessible windows—both inside and out. If desired, mix one part vinegar with three parts water to create your own window-washing solution for student use. Squeaky clean!

Cleaning Frenzy

Chances are, with sponges and cleaning solution in hand, youngsters will be transformed into live-action cleaning machines. To efficiently employ their cleaning urges, turn your students' efforts to the outdoor equipment and fixtures on your school grounds. While each youngster washes and scrubs the outdoor tables, playground equipment, and riding toys, encourage her to narrate her actions, using prepositions to describe her positional relationship to the object(s) being cleaned. Let the cleaning frenzy begin!

Ring Around The "Hosie"

Whew! If your youngsters have been busy bathing babies, doing the laundry, cleaning classroom items, washing cars and windows, and cleaning most everything else in sight, they must be ready for a bit of wet relaxation! Entice youngsters to cool their jets and just enjoy getting wet for the sake of getting wet with this idea. Set up a water sprinkler in a spacious outdoor area. Turn on the water; then bend and squeeze the hose leading to the sprinkler so that the water flow is interrupted. (Use a section of the hose far enough away so that you don't get wet yourself!) Invite youngsters to circle the sprinkler singing this song. On the last line of the song, release the hose so that the water flows to the sprinkler and a canopy of water results. Sip-sopping, drip-dropping wet is wonderful!

(sung to the tune of "Ring Around The Rosie")

Ring around the "hosie."
Pocket full of posies.
Water, water.
We all get wet!

19

Wet And Wonderful
Sensory Experiences

Try these sensory-stimulating activities to give youngsters still more reasons to get wet!

Piggies In The Puddle

A sensory treat awaits your little ones with this muddy listening game. To prepare a mud puddle, cover the bottom of a wading pool with purchased potting soil or topsoil; then mix water with the soil until it reaches a thick, soupy consistency. To play, ask a small group of students to role-play little pigs. Explain that when pigs get hot, they cool off by wallowing in mud. Then have the pigs circle around the mud puddle as you recite the rhyme below. Fill in the blank at the end of the rhyme, prompting youngsters to respond appropriately. Continue the game, providing a different response at the end of the rhyme each time so that every student has the opportunity to get in the mud. After the game, have students hose themselves clean. Aaahh, cool mud.

Hot little piggies circle round and round.
Into the mud you go if your name starts with this sound:
[sound/letter].

Slime Time, Rhyme Time

Help youngsters slime into some "ooey-gooey" rhyming practice with this activity. To begin, divide your class into pairs of students. Instruct each student pair to create slime by mixing one cup of water, two cups of cornstarch, and a small amount of green washable paint in a plastic container. If necessary, add small amounts of water to the slime until a thick, soupy consistency is achieved. Then ask a child in each pair to name a body part. Challenge her partner to say or create a corresponding rhyming word; then invite each child to rub a bit of slime on the named part of her body. Repeat the procedure, having the partners switch roles so that they take turns naming a body part, then a rhyming word. After each pair has become all slimed out or rhymed out, hose the slime off each student with a spray of water.

Sticking Together

If the names of their body parts just won't stick in students' memories, here's a cooperative game that might help. To begin, spray a large quantity of shaving cream into several large tubs to represent glue; then randomly place the tubs in a spacious outdoor area. To play, repeat the name of a body part to create a rhythmic chant. Have youngsters move around the play area, chorally repeating the chant while tapping that body part on themselves. On the signal, "Stick!", each youngster will find a partner, then scoop out a dollop of glue from the nearest tub. Each partner will rub glue on herself at the named body part; then she will "stick" herself to her partner's glued body part. For example, each student pair might be stuck together elbow-to-elbow or ankle-to-ankle. To separate the stuck-together students, spray a shower of water over each pair to wash away the glue. Then repeat the game, chanting the name of another body part.

Swamp Stomp

Conclude this sensory section with a good old-fashioned swamp stomp. To create a swamp, arrange an obstacle course to include the mud-filled pool from "Piggies In The Puddle" and a large tub of slime from "Slime Time, Rhyme Time" on page 20. Also position one or more large containers of the shaving-cream glue from "Sticking Together" in the obstacle course. Place a water sprinkler at the end of the swamp course. Tell youngsters that each sensory substance represents a swamp texture. For example, the mud might represent swamp mud (of course!) while the green slime might be swamp scum. The shaving-cream glue might be swamp foam and the spray from the water sprinkler swamp mist. Explain the path of the swamp stomp, including such actions as swimming through the swamp mud, splashing through the swamp scum, and wading through the swamp foam. Then invite each child, in turn, to negotiate his way through the murky, mushy swamp—completing the course with a grand-finale swamp stomp dance through the swamp mist. A swampy delight!

Cool 'Em Down

Is it just too hot for your little ones to enjoy the wet, sensory activities in this section? If so, cool 'em down with ice. Simply add ice to the mud puddle from "Piggies In The Puddle" and the slime mixture from "Slime Time, Rhyme Time" on page 20. If desired, also drop a few ice cubes into each tub of shaving-cream glue in "Sticking Together." Before long all your students will agree: It's cool to get wet!

Sponge Fun
Like sponges soak up water, youngsters will soak up the learning in these activities!

Lifestyle Of A Sponge

From general use and water play, students are most likely familiar with the water-retention and expansion properties of sponges. But have they ever really *thought* about the properties of a water-filled sponge versus a dried or wrung-out sponge? Try this activity to absorb youngsters' thoughts as well as to offer them some creative movement opportunities. Partially fill a wading pool with water; then show your class a dry sponge. Pass the sponge from child to child, encouraging each student to note its size, weight, and texture. Then have a volunteer dip an identical sponge into the pool of water. Ask him to wring the water out of the sponge. Prompt students to describe their observations about the changes the sponge undergoes.

Then saturate the imaginations of your students! To begin, have them curl up their bodies very tightly as if they were dry sponges; then ask them to imagine that they have just been immersed in water. Suggest that students unfold and stretch their bodies as big as possible, similar to water-filled sponges. Then challenge them to imitate sponges having the water wrung from them. After several rounds of this imaginary exercise, invite each youngster, in turn, to step into the pool and once again imagine he is a sponge—this time in real water.

Just Sponging Around!
Students will absorb a lot of skills practice while enjoying this assortment of wet sponge activities.

- Have a student pair transfer water from a bucket to a smaller container via a sponge, counting the number of sponge-wringings it takes to fill the smaller container.
- Invite student partners to toss a saturated sponge back and forth to each other.
- Encourage youngsters to toss soaked sponges at a target.
- Challenge each student to create a sidewalk or pavement design from the drippings of a squeezed sponge.
- Invite each youngster to use wet sponges to clap out a soggy rhythm.

We're going out to get wet.
Buckets of fun, you bet!
Splish, splish, splash, splash.
Soaking wet in a flash!

Date: _____

Place: _____

We're planning some wet, wonderful fun! Please send the following items for your child on the date above. And why not plan to beat the heat yourself? Just slip into your swimsuit and come join us!

_____ swimsuit
_____ bath towel
_____ sunscreen
_____ sunglasses

_____ change of clothes
_____ flip-flops or water shoes (optional)
_____ large, resealable plastic bag (for wet clothes)

©1997 The Education Center, Inc. • JULY • TEC757

Dear Parent,

Our class needs your help with a regatta (that's a special word for boat races) planned for _____. Please take time
(date)
with your child to create a boat for our regatta. The boat could be made of something as simple as a plastic soda bottle or a foam meat tray with a paper sail. After you and your child complete the boat, test it in a tub of water or a wading pool to make sure it floats. Then send the boat to school with your child on or before the regatta date. Have fun!

Thanks for your support,

_____
(teacher)

©1997 The Education Center, Inc. • JULY • TEC757

25

On The Lookout For A Cookout!

Summertime is the perfect time for a cookout. So fire up students' appetites for learning with this tasty thematic unit.

ideas contributed by Vicki Mockaitis Pacchetti

Barbecue Brainstorm

Get your cookout unit off to a hot start by gathering your little ones together for a mouthwatering discussion about this tasty topic. In advance cut a hamburger patty from brown construction paper and two bun halves from tan construction paper. Glue the three pieces of paper together to resemble a hamburger as shown. Mount the cutout onto a flat surface such as your easel or a bulletin board. During group time, ask student volunteers what types of foods are cooked on grills. Write students' responses on the giant hamburger. Then have students share other words and phrases associated with cookouts and barbecues. Responses might include cookout tools, games, or paper products. After recording these responses, display the hamburger cutout on a classroom wall.

hot dogs   napkins
paper plates   smoke
potato chips   ketchup
picnic table   hamburgers
grill   potato salad

Singing Chefs

What's the next best thing to having a cookout? Singing about one! In advance bring in a toy grill. Or create a pretend grill by placing a wire baking rack atop a cardboard box. If desired, add rocks or spray-paint Styrofoam® balls black to resemble charcoal; then place them in the box. Gather students in a circle around the grill and teach them this summertime tune and its accompanying movements.

Let's All Have A Cookout Today
(sung to the tune of "Here We Go 'Round The Mulberry Bush")

Let's all have a cookout today, a cookout today,
    a cookout today.
Let's all have a cookout today, and fun in the summer sun.

Clap hands to each beat.

There's the grill that cooks the food, cooks the food,
    cooks the food.
There's the grill that cooks the food; that's how the food gets done.

Point to the grill.

Flip the burgers and the hot dogs, and the hot dogs,
    and the hot dogs.
Flip the burgers and the hot dogs—enough for
    everyone.

Pretend to flip a burger with a spatula.

Gather the chips, dips, and your friends, and your friends,
    and your friends.
Gather the chips, dips, and your friends, and let's all eat
    a ton...MUNCH!

Signal "come here" with your hands.

Pretend to take a huge bite.

We're Having A Cookout

Play this fun memory game with your little ones, and watch their excitement for cookouts grow! (This game also makes a great lead-in to the next activity, "All Decked Out For Dramatic Play.") To prepare for the game, bring in a large cooler and a variety of cookout items, such as plastic squeeze bottles for ketchup and mustard, a checkered vinyl tablecloth, tongs, a spatula, an apron, plastic or paper plates and cups, plastic utensils, and napkins. Place the cookout items in the cooler and have a small group of students form a circle around the cooler. Begin by having a student choose a cookout item from the cooler and say, "We're having a cookout, and I brought the [cookout item]." The student then returns with his cookout item to his spot in the circle. Then invite another student to choose an item from the cooler. Have him repeat the first child's sentence, and add the name of his own cookout item. Continue until each child has had a turn. Encourage students to look at the items in their classmates' hands to help them remember the previous items listed.

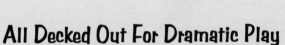

All Decked Out For Dramatic Play

Transform your dramatic-play area into a deck or patio to encourage role-playing throughout your cookout unit. Stock the area with the props and cooler used in "We're Having A Cookout," a pretend grill (see "Singing Chefs" on page 26), and some child-size lounge chairs, a petite picnic table, or a blanket or two spread on the floor. Also gather an assortment of plastic cookout-type food, or cut sponges or felt to resemble hot dogs and hamburgers. Encourage children playing in the area to use the cookout items and foods as they have their own cookout. Now, who wants burgers and hot dogs?

27

Hamburger Patterns

Cook up some patterning practice with this appetizing activity. In advance duplicate several copies of the burger ingredients on page 30 for each student. Then cut a 4" x 18" strip of construction paper for each child. Distribute the burger patterns and a strip to each student. Have each student color and cut out her burger ingredients. Then challenge each child to use the cutouts to create a repetitive pattern, such as *lettuce, tomato, cheese, lettuce, tomato, cheese.* After checking each child's pattern, have her glue her cutouts to her construction-paper strip. Voila—patterns that look good enough to eat!

Build A Burger

Build basic-skills knowledge with this small-group activity. Duplicate, color, and cut out several sets of the burger ingredients on page 30. Mount each picture on a piece of tagboard; then laminate the pictures for durability. Label the pieces in each set with numerals, shapes, or letters; then place each set in a resealable plastic bag. (Each bag will have two buns, one patty, a piece of lettuce, a piece of cheese, and a tomato slice.)

To begin the game, distribute a bag to each student in the group and have him empty it in front of him. Then—depending on the skill you choose—announce a shape, letter, numeral, or beginning sound and have each child search for a match on his burger ingredients. If a child has a match, he places that piece to the side. Play continues in this same manner as each student uses his matches to build a stacked burger. The first student to have six matches (and a stacked burger), announces, "I built a burger!" Continue play until each child has built his burger. Change skills on the game pieces by wiping off the original programming with a spritz of hairspray.

One-Of-A-Kind Burgers

Encourage your young chefs to try their spatulas at creating their own burger recipes—the crazier, the better! Will it be a chocolate-pickle burger or a rose-petal burger? After each child has decided on the ingredients for her burger, give her a sheet of paper and have her illustrate her burger. Then write each child's dictation describing her burger on her individual page. Compile all the recipes into a class book titled "One-Of-A-Kind Burgers." Then share this class menu and listen to your hungry ones giggle for more!

Hot Potato—Cookout Style

Play this cookout version of Hot Potato to sharpen students' gross-motor skills. In advance ask each child to bring an oven mitt to school. (Be sure to locate some extra mitts in case some students forget.) You will also need an uncooked potato and some aluminum foil. Gather students in a circle and place the pretend grill from "Singing Chefs" (page 26) in the middle of the circle. Explain to your youngsters that some people wrap food in foil before placing it on a grill. Then wrap the potato in foil and place it on the pretend grill. While the potato is "cooking," have students put on their oven mitts. Once the potato is "hot," play a selection of music and send the potato around the circle. Remind each student that since the potato is "hot," he can touch it only with his hand that's wearing the mitt. At random intervals, stop the music and send the student holding the potato to the middle of the circle until the next round. Briefly "reheat" the potato and begin play again.

Hamburger Cookies

Conclude your cookout unit with this delicious burger-making experience.

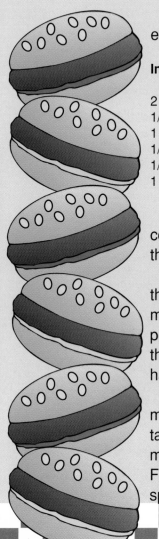

Ingredients For Patties (makes 25–30):

2 Tbs. cocoa
1/4 cup milk
1 cup sugar`
1/4 cup butter
1/4 cup peanut butter
1 cup uncooked oatmeal

Ingredients For One Cookie:

2 vanilla wafers
1 Tbs. patty mixture
vanilla ready-to-spread frosting
yellow and red food coloring
sesame seeds
water

In advance divide the frosting into three small jars. Use food coloring to color one-third red (ketchup) and one-third yellow (mustard). Leave one-third white (mayonnaise). Place a plastic knife beside each jar.

Prepare the patty mixture using a pot and a portable burner. Stir together the cocoa and the milk. Add the sugar and the butter, and boil about three minutes. Add the peanut butter and the uncooked oatmeal; then stir until the peanut butter has melted. Remove from heat and stir until mixture begins to thicken. Allow the mixture to cool slightly; then have students make their hamburger cookies while the patty mixture is still pliable.

To make a hamburger cookie, a student chooses and spreads the condiments she wants on the flat side of one vanilla wafer. Next she forms a tablespoon of the patty mixture into a patty, stacks the patty atop the condiments, and then tops the make-believe burger with the other vanilla wafer. Finally she dampens the top vanilla wafer with a wet paper towel and sprinkles a small spoonful of sesame seeds on it. Ready for a bite?

Burger Ingredients
Use with "Hamburger Patterns" and "Build A Burger" on page 28.

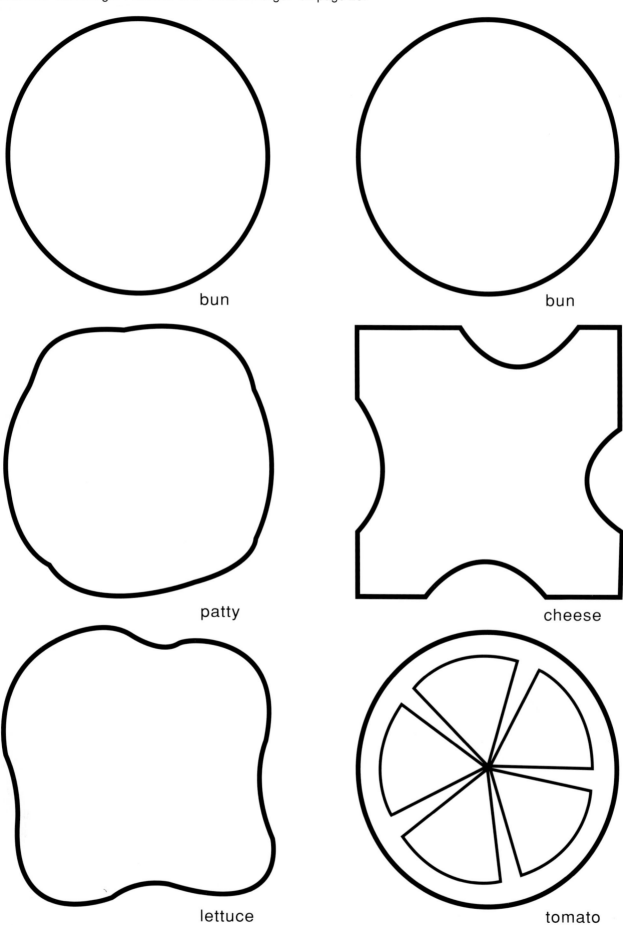

bun

bun

patty

cheese

lettuce

tomato

Everybody's Yellin' For Watermelon!

This juicy assortment of watermelon activities will have youngsters' mouths watering. Have fun serving up this favorite slice of summer!

ideas contributed by Lucia Kemp Henry and Angie Kutzer

Guess What?

Begin the melon madness by having your little ones play the parts of supersleuths. Hide a watermelon in a box. On the outside of the box, write clues describing the watermelon. During circle time, show the box to your students and read the clues aloud. Invite volunteers to guess what's inside. After all guesses have been made, unveil the mighty melon. As an extension, challenge older students to list other descriptive words or phrases for a watermelon.

Oval shape, hard outside, soft inside, crunchy, has stripes

We are family...

Melon Mania

Watermelons aren't the only ones! The other members in their gourd family include muskmelons, pumpkins, squash, cucumbers, and zucchini. Haul an example of each of these gourds into the classroom for older students to compare, contrast, and examine. Or, for younger children, bring in the three most common melons—a watermelon, cantaloupe, and honeydew—for comparison. Call attention to the color(s), pattern, smell, and texture of the outside of each melon; then slice each one in half to investigate the inside. They're all melons and/or gourds, yet each has its own unique characteristics, just like us!

Juicy, Juicy, Juicy

Use the three cut melons from "Melon Mania" to give youngsters' taste buds a treat. Cover one half of each melon with plastic wrap and place it near a piece of paper labeled with its name. Then cut the other half of each melon into bite-sized cubes, saving the watermelon seeds for later. Put each melon's pieces into a separate bowl and place each bowl beside the corresponding covered melon half. Invite each child to sample the melons. Then have her vote for her favorite by placing a sticker on the paper that's labeled with her choice. Tally the votes with your students by counting the stickers aloud. Have a volunteer report the winning melon. For older youngsters, you may want to graph the data on a picture or bar graph. Before putting away the covered melon halves for another snacktime, take a photo of each child holding the watermelon to use in the booklet described on page 32 (see "A Slice Of Reading"). Conclude this juicy activity by reading *Anansi And The Talking Melon* retold by Eric A. Kimmel (Holiday House, Inc.).

Watermelon

That Wonderful Watermelon!

Help your youngsters learn this short fingerplay to introduce them to the parts of a watermelon.

A watermelon is round
And as hard as your head.
The *rind* is green,
And the *flesh* is red.

Make a circle with arms and hands.
"Knock" lightly on head with fist.
Clasp hands together to show melon.
Open hands to show melon's inside.

A watermelon tastes good
And is a juicy treat.
But the *seeds* inside,
You do not eat.

Take a bite from a pretend melon slice.
Rub tummy.
Point to the inside of cupped hand.
Shake head "no."

The seeds.

The flesh.

The rind.

Mighty fine!

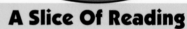

A Slice Of Reading

Review the parts of a watermelon with this slice of summer reading. For each child, cut one green construction-paper semicircle at least eight inches long on the straight side. Then cut a slightly smaller semicircle from red construction paper and an even smaller semicircle from laminating scraps or transparency film. Then assemble a watermelon slice by stapling the semicircles together as shown. Working with one small group at a time, invite each child to use a permanent black marker to draw seeds on the clear layer of her watermelon slice. Then circulate and ask each child to name the parts of the melon as you point them out: *seeds, flesh,* and *rind.* Use a black permanent marker to label each layer of the watermelon as shown.

When a youngster has successfully named all the watermelon parts, flip her watermelon slice over and print the words "Mighty fine!" on the back. Then present the photo taken of her during "Juicy, Juicy, Juicy" on page 31 and have her glue it above the text. (Or have her illustrate a picture of herself eating watermelon in the available space.) Encourage little ones to take these simple-to-read slices home to show off their knowledge for their families. What a way to ripen beginning reading skills!

A Watermelon Tree?

Why not? Celebrate summer with a classroom tree loaded with these watermelon ornaments. Give each youngster half of a large Styrofoam® ball. Have him paint the rounded side green and the flat side red. If desired, spray the dried paint with a layer of clear gloss. After the gloss is dry, direct the child to glue on a few real watermelon seeds. Then insert a green pipe cleaner, as shown, and twist the end to make a hook for hanging. Let each child hang his summertime delight on a tree branch placed in a gravel-filled flowerpot. What a sight for summer eyes!

Works Of "W-art-ermelon"

Decorate your room with these wild and wacky works of art. Give each child a large sheet of white construction paper. Provide two shades of green paint and brushes for each child to paint a large rind on her paper. Then give choices for filling in the fleshy part of the melon—for example, red fingerpaint, crayon, colored chalk, sponge paint, tissue paper, or even lipstick! For even more fun, explain to your little ones that watermelon flesh can actually be white, yellow, orange, or pink, depending on the variety. Then give youngsters even more colorful options for completing their slices. When the materials used on the artwork are dry, have each child glue on real seeds or black construction-paper dots from a hole puncher. Hang these melons on the wall or in the hall, but be careful—they're awfully juicy!

Allison

Stephen

Fine-Motor Melon

Put clean, leftover watermelon seeds to good use in this fine-motor activity. For each child, duplicate a watermelon slice on white construction paper from the pattern on page 35. Have him color his melon slice; then use a marker to write a large *W* in the center. Encourage him to trace the letter with glue, then add watermelon seeds to cover the glue lines. If desired, cut out each child's melon and use it as a front cover for a book of words that begin with *W*. Worms and whales and watches, oh my!

Watermelon Puzzlers

Duplicate an even number of watermelon slices from the pattern on page 35 onto white construction paper. Color the rinds green and the centers of the slices red. Cut out all the slices and mount half of them onto separate pieces of construction paper. Laminate the melon cards and the remaining slices for durability. Then cut the remaining slices so that each one fits together in a unique way. Vary the number of pieces according to the abilities in your group. Insert one melon card and one cut-up melon slice into a resealable plastic bag to make a puzzle kit. These puzzles serve up lots of fun, no matter how you slice 'em!

Just "Ripe" For Review

Gather your little ones around this watermelon patch for a rollicking review of basic skills. To prepare, duplicate a large supply of the watermelon slice pattern on page 35 onto green construction paper. Cut out the slices and—if desired—color the flesh red and use a black crayon to draw lines across the back of the pattern to resemble the outside of a watermelon. Then label each slice with a letter, a numeral, a sight word, a colored dot, a shape, or another skill you'd like reinforced. (For older students you may even want to mix skills together.) Spread the cutouts on the floor, facedown, along with strands of green curly-ribbon "vines" to make a big watermelon patch. Choose a few volunteers to walk around the patch while the rest of the group chants the following rhyme. When the rhyme ends, have each volunteer pick a melon and tell what is found on the "inside." If she is correct, reward her with a watermelon-flavored treat, such as jelly beans, and have her pick someone to take her place in the patch. If she is incorrect, have her stay in the patch until she finds a melon that's just "ripe"!

Watermelon, watermelon, watermelon rind.
Pick one up and tell us what you find!

Triangle.

A Behavior "In-seed-tive"

Keep your classroom juicy all summer long by using seedless watermelon-slice cutouts to encourage appropriate behavior. Personalize a cutout for each student. Allow her to either glue a real watermelon seed or add an inked fingerprint "seed" to her slice for each day of good behavior. When a designated number of seeds have been accumulated, reward her with a watermelon-flavored or watermelon-scented treat.

Rachel

Watermelon Slice Pattern

Use with "Fine-Motor Melon" on page 33 and "Watermelon Puzzlers" and "Just 'Ripe' For Review" on page 34.

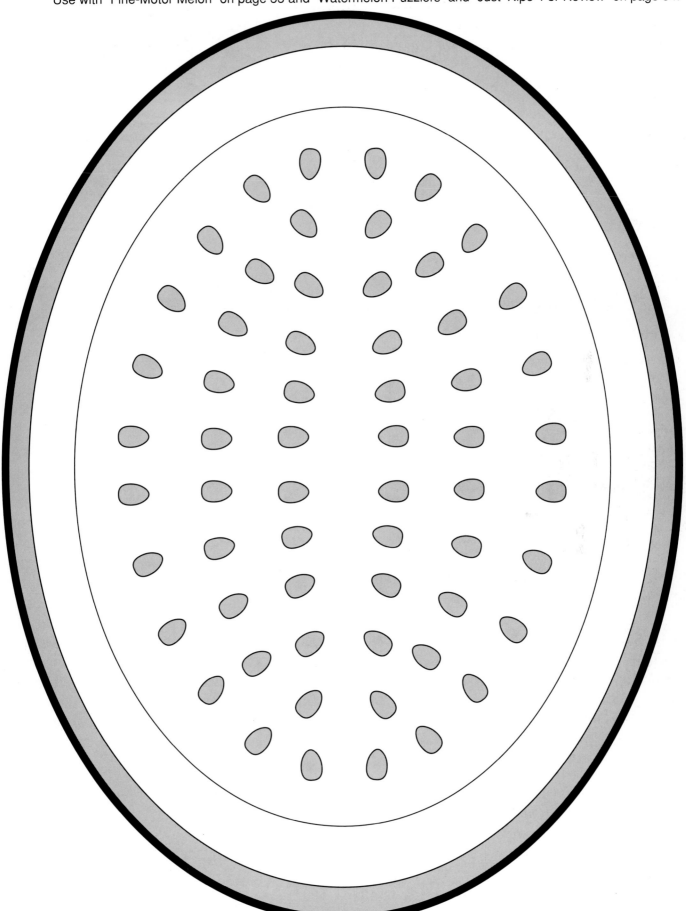

OPPOSITES MARCH

Give students opportunities to practice matching opposites with this group game. Duplicate a set of the opposites cards (pages 42–43) onto tagboard; then color and cut out all the cards. Laminate the cards if desired. Position three Hula-Hoops® on the floor; then label one "the sun" and another "the moon." Randomly place the opposites cards inside these two hoops. Invite a student to choose a card from a hoop, then name the concept shown on her card. Select a volunteer to look for the corresponding opposite card. Instruct her to march around the hoops, as you lead the class in singing the song below. When the child finds the matching opposite card, invite her to name the concept. Instruct both children to place the matching pair inside the third hoop. Continue play until each child has had an opportunity to make a pair.

(sung to the tune of "Sally Go 'Round The Sun")
[Child's name] go 'round the sun.
[Child's name] go 'round the moon.
[Child's name] go find the opposite.
And show it to the group.

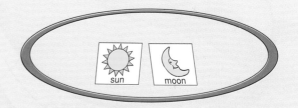

FLIPPING FOR OPPOSITES

Emergent readers will flip for these fun books. To make one, duplicate the booklet backing (page 45) onto tagboard. Cut six 4 1/2" x 3 1/2" pieces of newsprint. Stack three pieces; then staple them along the left side of the booklet backing. Staple the remaining newsprint rectangles along the right side. Display the opposites cards used in "Opposites March" in your writing center. Have a child choose pairs of opposites. Instruct him to illustrate one concept from a pair on the left side of his booklet, and the corresponding opposite on the right side of his booklet. Encourage more advanced students to label their illustrations with the appropriate opposite words. Repeat the steps until all the pages are illustrated. Have each child share his booklet with you. When he reaches the last page, program the award on the booklet backing with his name. Send the booklets home so youngsters can share their knowledge of opposites with their families.

HAND JIVE

Get little ones movin' and groovin' to the opposites beat with this hip hand jive! Have students alternate hand claps and leg slaps as you lead them in the following rhyme. Then, as little ones become familiar with this rhyme, instruct them to shout out the missing word as you omit the second word in each pair.

Night, day,
Whisper, shout,
Push, pull,
In and out.

On, off,
Left, right,
Dirty, clean,
Dim and bright.

Nice, mean,
Wet, dry,
Near, far,
Low and high.

Big, small,
Smile, frown,
Over, under,
Up and down!

Small!

Clevell Harris

EDIBLE OPPOSITES

Put youngsters' opposites knowledge to the test—taste test, that is—with this delicious treat. To make one, spread peanut butter (smooth) onto a toasted English muffin (rough), top with banana slices (soft), and sprinkle with mini chocolate chips (hard). Mmm…good!

ROLLING OPPOSITES

You'll see lots of smiley faces when kindergartners participate in this prediction activity. In advance spray-paint a quantity of lima beans yellow; then allow them to dry. Use a fine-tip black permanent marker to program one side of each bean with a smiley face and the other side with a sad face. Then duplicate the recording sheet on page 44 for each child. Provide each child with a recording sheet, a small plastic cup, and a decorated bean. Instruct him to predict the number of smiley faces that he will roll after rolling the bean ten times. Have him write the numeral where indicated. Instruct each student to place his bean inside the cup, then gently roll it out. Have him record the results on his sheet by coloring in an appropriate bean. After ten rolls, instruct youngsters to count the total number of smiley faces and sad faces they rolled. Discuss and compare the results. Did anyone predict correctly?

Adapt this activity for preschoolers by having each child roll his decorated bean ten times. Have him record the results of each roll by coloring in an appropriate bean on his recording sheet. After ten rolls assist him in counting the number of happy and sad faces he rolled.

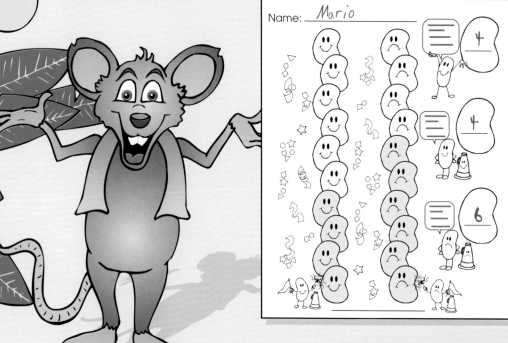

CRAZY OPPOSITES DAY

We will be having a crazy opposites day on ___July 16___. Please send your child to school that day wearing opposites. This fun-filled learning day is sure to be the opposite of ordinary!

CRAZY OPPOSITES DAY

Culminate your opposites unit by having a Crazy Opposites Day. Send home a copy of the parent letter on page 45 with each child. On the scheduled day, encourage each student to show off her own opposite pairs during a group time. Throughout the day—at unexpected times—give a direction or make a statement using the opposite of a word that is typically used in context. For example, you might say, "It's time to go *inside* for recess." Express your appreciation to those students who correct your statements by commenting on how well they listen and think about the words they hear. Don't forget to tell them, "Please!"

40

SING A SONG OF OPPOSITES

Reinforce opposites concepts with one or more of these musical selections.

"Song About Slow, Song About Fast"
Walter The Waltzing Worm
Sung by Hap Palmer
Educational Activities, Inc.

"Say The Opposite"
Can A Cherry Pie Wave Goodbye?
Sung by Hap Palmer
Hap Pal Music, Inc.

"The Freeze"
We All Live Together, Vol. 2
Sung by Greg & Steve
Youngheart Records

UP AND DOWN, BOOKS ALL AROUND

Language opportunities will abound when you place some of these books about opposites in your library area.

The Lifesize Animal Opposites Book
Written by Lee Davis
Published by Dorling Kindersley Publishing, Inc.

Popposites
Designed by Jung-Huyn Yoon
Published by Dorling Kindersley Publishing, Inc.

Push, Pull, Empty, Full: A Book Of Opposites
Written by Tana Hoban
Published By Simon & Schuster Books For
    Young Readers

What's The Opposite? A Lift-The-Flap Book
Written by Eric Hill
Published By Puffin Books

Opposite Cards

Use with "Opposites March" and "Flipping For Opposites" on page 38.

sun	moon	empty
full	plain	fancy
big	little	open
front	back	shut

Opposite Cards

Use with "Opposites March" and "Flipping For Opposites" on page 38.

short

tall

curly

straight

awake

asleep

up

down

left

laugh

cry

right

Name: _____

How many smiley faces will I roll?

_____

I rolled smiley faces.

_____

I rolled sad faces.

_____

Note To The Teacher: Use with "Rolling Opposites" on page 40.

HOORAY!

_____
(child's name)

knows all about

Opposites!

©1997 The Education Center, Inc. • *JULY* • TEC757

Parent Letter
Use with "Crazy Opposites Day" on page 40.

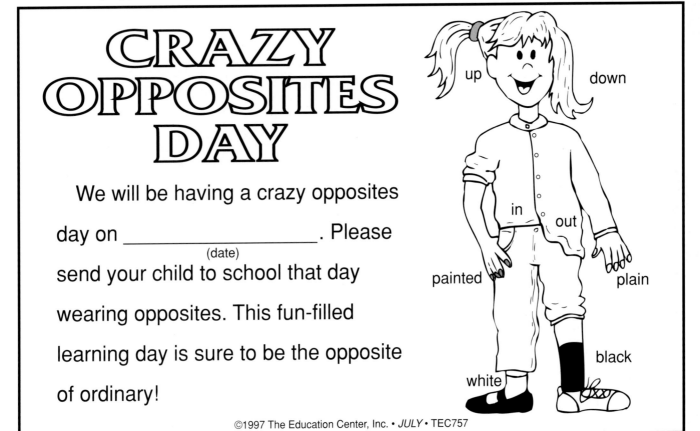

CRAZY OPPOSITES DAY

We will be having a crazy opposites

day on _____. Please
(date)

send your child to school that day

wearing opposites. This fun-filled

learning day is sure to be the opposite

of ordinary!

up   down

in   out

painted   plain

black

white

©1997 The Education Center, Inc. • *JULY* • TEC757

RAINY-DAY RESCUE!

Rescue students from the rainy-day blues with this collection of fun-filled activities that are sure to chase away the doldrums!

ideas contributed by Linda Gordetsky

COLOR QUEST

Add a little spark to a dreary rainy day with this colorful scavenger hunt. In advance prepare several different lists of colored items to be found in your classroom. Use markers to write the color words in the appropriate colors. Then divide your class into teams of four or five students each. Provide each team with a prepared list and a box in which to deposit its found items. Instruct each team to search the classroom for items in the colors on its list, then place the items in its box.

When a team has collected all the listed items, the members sit beside their box and each member raises his hand. Instruct the other teams to stop their searches while you verify the contents of the box. When you've determined that the team has completed its list, have the students remain seated; then instruct the other teams to continue their searches until each team has completed its list.

> 4 **red** things
> 2 **blue** things
> 3 **purple** things
> 1 **yellow** thing

A HUNT OF A DIFFERENT COLOR

When little ones are familiar with the concept of a scavenger hunt, try this more challenging hunt. Duplicate the form on page 52 and the pictures on page 53 for each team. Prepare a list for each team by cutting out an assortment of symbols from page 53, then gluing them in the boxes on the blank form. Be careful to vary the order of the symbols so that each team is not hunting for the same item at the same time. Begin the scavenger hunt by dividing students into teams of four or five students each. Provide each team with a list of items to be gathered. Explain to students that they will be hunting for items around your classroom according to categories indicated by the picture symbols. For example, a picture of food would instruct them to find a food item in the classroom—such as an item of play food from the housekeeping area. Or a picture of a pencil would tell them to find something to write with—such as a crayon or marker. After explaining the meaning of the symbols, conduct the hunt as described in "Color Quest."

ALL ABOUT WEATHER

46

UNDER COVER

This game is sure to have your little puddle jumpers running for cover! To begin, brainstorm with students a list of outdoor activities they enjoy on a sunny day. Write their responses on a sheet of chart paper. Then ask volunteers to suggest things that they do when it starts to rain. When students come to the conclusion that they usually seek shelter, teach them the Summer Showers game.

To prepare, remove chairs and stack them away from tables to provide safe shelter in your classroom. Then play some lively calypso music or other summertime music in the background as you name an activity from the chart. Invite students to dramatize the suggested activity while the music is playing. When the music stops, challenge students to find shelter under a table. Ready…set…don't get wet!

- playing on the swings
- going to the pool
- having a picnic
- running with my dog
- playing in the water sprinkler
- waiting for the ice cream man

RAINING ON THE INSIDE

It's raining, it's pouring; but it's nice and dry in the classroom—or is it? This simple demonstration will help youngsters visualize how raindrops form. In a lidded quart jar, pour enough warm water to cover the bottom. Turn the lid upside down and position it atop the mouth of the jar. Place a few ice cubes inside the lid; then leave the jar untouched for several minutes. After several minutes, instruct youngsters to carefully observe the underside of the jar lid to see the tiny drops of water that have formed.

Explain to students that some of the water in the bottom of the jar *evaporated* and changed into a gas called *vapor*. The water vapor turned back into water as it touched the cool jar lid, forming drops. Relate this to the rain outside by explaining that on earth, water from rivers, lakes, and oceans evaporates and travels into the air as water vapor. When the water vapor reaches the cooler upper atmosphere (the clouds), it returns to liquid in the form of raindrops.

Finish up this activity by having the group make an experience chart depicting the experiment. Or simply invite younger children to draw rainy-day scenes while you play some soothing music.

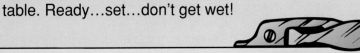

IT'S RAINING...BROCCOLI?

Weather-weary students will soon forget the conditions outside when you entertain them with a hilarious book! Read aloud *Cloudy With A Chance Of Meatballs* by Judith Barrett (Atheneum Books For Young Readers); then invite your young gourmets to concoct a "chow-showered" town of their own. Visually divide a length of bulletin-board paper into seven sections; then label each section with a different day of the week. Invite youngsters to illustrate the bottom of each section of the paper with houses, stores, and people. Next have students cut out magazine pictures of different types of food, and place them in a box. During a group time, invite students to help sort the pictures into seven groups—such as fruits, vegetables, meats, grains, beverages, sweets, and dairy foods. Finally, encourage students to glue each group of pictures to a section of the bulletin-board paper to resemble rain. Display the completed mural on a wall or in a hallway near your classroom.

MUNCHY, CRUNCHY MINIBOOKS

If your students enjoy the story extension in "It's Raining…Broccoli?", then you'll be amazed to see what's raining from the pages of these student-created minibooks. Duplicate and cut out a set of minibook pages (pages 54 and 55) for each child. To make a book, have a child either draw pictures of food, or cut out and glue food pictures from magazines to illustrate each page. When her pages are complete, write her dictated ending to the sentence on each page. Sequence the pages; then staple them between construction-paper covers. Encourage each child to dictate a title for her minibook. Have each child share her finished book with a classmate before taking it home.

SAVING FOR A RAINY DAY

Be prepared for any rainy day by gathering a collection of board games. Enlist the help of parents by sending home a copy of the parent letter (page 52) with each child. Then prepare a special place for the games by concealing a shelf with a curtain. To make one, measure a length of fabric (or bulletin-board paper) equal to the length of your shelf. Decorate the fabric with rainy-day symbols—such as umbrellas, clouds, raindrops, and lightning bolts—using permanent markers. Attach the hook side of a length of adhesive Velcro® to the shelf. Attach the loop side of the Velcro® to the curtain; then press the curtain onto the shelf. As the games arrive, tuck them away behind the curtain. Now, when a rainy day washes away your outdoor play time, indoor play will be cozy and educational.

B-BOPPIN' BALLOONS

Students will be hoping for more rainy days after this balloon-bop bash! Seat youngsters in a circle; then invite a pair of students to stand and attempt to keep a balloon afloat. Instruct each student to use her open hand as a racquet. (Or make racquets ahead of time by stretching the leg from a pair of panty hose over a shaped metal clothes hanger.) When a child misses the balloon, instruct her to choose another student to bop the balloon, then sit down. Continue to play until each child has had an opportunity to play. The last child to remain standing is named the "Big Bopper!"

RAINY-DAY OBSTACLE COURSE

Don't let the rain be an obstacle to gross-motor fun! Prepare an indoor obstacle course to help release rainy-day wiggles. Arrange cones, furniture, Hula-Hoops®, and gym equipment around your classroom to create an obstacle course. Explain the sequence of the course—such as walk between the cones, crawl under the table, jump into each hoop, walk across the balance beam, bounce the ball to the mat, and then jump over the mat. Invite a volunteer to maneuver his way through the obstacle course as you explain each section. Then give each student an opportunity to complete the course. Vary the course by inviting pairs of children to complete the course together.

Scavenger Hunt Form

Use with "A Hunt Of A Different Color" on page 46.

1.	2.	3.
4.	5.	6.

Parent Letter

Use with "Saving For A Rainy Day" on page 49.

Dear Family,

Board games are great learning tools for the rainy days just around the corner. We would greatly appreciate your help in collecting a variety of games for classroom use. If you have some old games tucked away on a toy shelf, we would be happy to recycle them for our classroom's rainy-day collection. With your help our collection will grow, and your next spring cleaning will be a bit easier!

Thanks for your help,

_____

something to eat

something to build with

something you use for counting

something you measure with

something you wear

something you throw

something you read

something to write with

something that makes music

In our town of

_____,

strange weather was known
to occur.

©1997 The Education Center, Inc. • *JULY* • TEC757

1

On Sunday, it rained

_____.

2

On Monday, it rained

_____.

3

On Tuesday, it rained

_____.

4

Minibook Pages
Use with "Munchy, Crunchy Minibooks" on page 48.

On Wednesday, it rained

_____.

5

On Thursday, it rained

_____.

6

On Friday, it rained

_____.

7

On Saturday, it rained

_____.

8

Traveling Tots

Summertime means vacation time for many families. Whether it's a trip to the mountains, a trek to the lake, a week at Grandma's house, or a few quiet days at home, vacations provide memories that can last a lifetime. Capitalize on the excitement surrounding summer vacations by planning a unit that will have little ones cruising along on a learning adventure. Let's go!

ideas contributed by Barbara Backer

Timely Tips

Remind parents about vacation safety and give them some tips for making travel with their little ones more enjoyable. Simply duplicate the letter on page 60 for each child to take home at the beginning of your unit. Mom and Dad will appreciate that you are interested in their child even when he's *not* at school!

A Traveling Exhibit

Prepare a bulletin-board display where youngsters can share their vacation memories. In advance collect travel brochures and pictures of varied vacation destinations from travel agencies, airlines, bus or train companies, travel magazines, or your local tourist bureau. Create a travel collage border around one of your bulletin boards. Add the title "How We Spent Our Summer Vacations." Then encourage youngsters to bring in photos, drawings, or travel memorabilia from their family vacations. Post some or all of the items on the board, along with children's dictation about their vacations. Leave the display up throughout the summer and add to it or change it as each child shares his vacation experiences.

Vacation Bound

Vacations provide three main topics for discussion: Where do people go? How do they get there? What do they do while they are there?

Cruise into your unit by creating a three-column chart on a large piece of bulletin-board paper. Label each column with one of the three questions about vacations. Then lead youngsters in a discussion about vacations, having them brainstorm ideas to fill in the chart. Provide markers, stickers, clip art, and magazine pictures; then have children illustrate the chart. Post the chart on a classroom wall and encourage youngsters to add new ideas as their families plan or return from vacations.

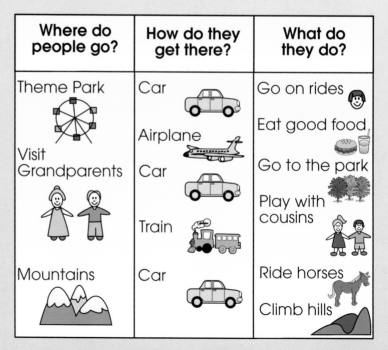

Where do people go?	How do they get there?	What do they do?
Theme Park	Car	Go on rides
	Airplane	Eat good food
Visit Grandparents	Car	Go to the park
	Train	Play with cousins
Mountains	Car	Ride horses / Climb hills

Travelin' Along, Singin' A Song

Teach youngsters the first verse of this song. Then encourage a volunteer to name a destination to complete the second verse of the song and an activity to complete the third verse. Repeat the song as many times as desired, having other students suggest destinations and activities. Encourage youngsters to add movements to dramatize their chosen method of travel and to act out their vacation activities.

We're Going On A Vacation
(sung to the tune of "Do You Know The Muffin Man?")

We're going on a vacation,
A vacation, a vacation.
We're going on a vacation,
And this is where we'll go.

We're going to [the fishing lake]
[The fishing lake, the fishing lake].
We're going to [the fishing lake]
And this is what we'll do.

We'll [catch a really big fish]
[A big fish, a big fish].
We'll [catch a really big fish]
When we are at [the lake].

Vacation Memories Of A Different Sort

This activity is packed with visual-memory skills. In advance bring in a small suitcase and a variety of items you might take on a trip—such as a shampoo bottle, sunglasses, a book, a travel brochure, and an old airline ticket. At circle time, invite a child to name each item, then pack it in the suitcase while her classmates watch carefully. Then have her take the suitcase behind a screen or bookshelf and instruct her to remove one item from the bag. Ask her to bring the suitcase back to the circle area and open it. Can anyone name the missing item? Continue the game by having other children take turns packing and removing items from the suitcase. Increase the number of items in the bag as your students' visual memory improves.

Destination: Learning Centers

Transform your classroom into a vacationer's paradise! Provide props in various learning centers to stimulate children's vacation play. Use these suggestions to get started; then encourage your students to think of other items, or shop local garage sales for even more ideas.

Dramatic-Play Area: Add suitcases; old airline, bus, or train tickets; empty sunscreen bottles; sunglasses; hats; beach towels; tickets or brochures from theme parks; cameras (without film); a magnetic fishing game; an empty cooler; or child-size backpacks. For added fun, designate a day for the whole class to pretend your classroom is a motel. Invite students to bring their pajamas to school. Set up resting mats or blankets on the floor to serve as beds. Ask parents for travel-size soaps and shampoo bottles. Bring a luggage rack from home. Order room service and have youngsters roll in a cart holding your snack. You might even set up a wading pool outside and encourage everyone to bring a swimsuit and take a dip!

Block Area: Add any travel-related items you may have from LEGO® sets, such as an airplane, a boat, a bus, a camper, or cars. Wooden or plastic people figures are a must. Encourage youngsters to use inclined blocks to make a boat ramp or mountain. A blue piece of cloth can serve as a lake or an ocean. Post pictures of airplanes, cruise ships, or travel posters to stimulate children's thinking.

Art/Writing Area: Include materials for making scrapbooks—such as paper, markers, scissors, glue, a stapler, and travel brochures. Encourage children's writing skills by providing stationery, envelopes, postcards, and cancelled postage stamps.

Snack Area: Youngsters will enjoy playing "flight attendant" in this center when you supply serving trays, paper cups, napkins, aprons, and snack-size packages of pretzels or nuts.

Keys To The Room

If your little ones love to play with keys, they'll enjoy this numeral-matching game. To prepare, search your house for ten old, unusable keys (or ask parents to donate them). Purchase some round, write-on key tags. Attach a tag to each key, and label each one with a different numeral from 1 to 10. Then gather ten sheets of construction paper. Decorate each sheet of paper to resemble a motel-room door, complete with a knob and a numeral from 1 to 10 written prominently on the front. Laminate the sheets for durability. To play the game, a child lays all ten doors faceup on a tabletop. He identifies the numeral on each door, then locates the key with the matching numeral on its label and lays it atop the door.

Increase the difficulty of the game for older children by labeling the doors and keys with numerals that will challenge their visual discrimination—such as *113, 131,* and *311.*

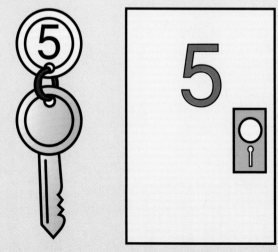

A Wild And Wacky Vacation

Most of your little ones will have a fun—but tame—time on their summer vacations. For some *real* excitement, share the silly story *How I Spent My Summer Vacation* by Mark Teague (Crown Publishers, Inc.). In this book a young boy tells the outlandish story of how he was captured by cowboys on the way to his Aunt Fern's house. After sharing the story, invite the class to make up a creative story about a wild and wacky vacation. Begin by having youngsters brainstorm ideas as you jot them down on a sheet of chart paper. Help the children compose a group story. When they are satisfied with the story, write a clean version on large sheets of construction paper and have students illustrate it. Gather the pages, create a cover, and staple the book together. Add the book to your classroom library or send it home with a different child each night so youngsters can share it with their families.

The school bus turned into a rocket. The kids in Miss Wilson's class were going into outer space!

Vacation Reading

Add any or all of these books to your reading center or storytime to extend your youngsters' familiarity with vacation experiences.

A Big Trip For The Morrisons
Written by Penny Carter
Published by Viking

The Bag I'm Taking To Grandma's
Written by Shirley Neitzel
Published by Greenwillow Books

Patch Takes A Vacation
Written by Jo Lodge
Published by Red Wagon Books

Those Summers
Written by Aliki
Published by HarperCollins Publishers

The Brass Ring
Written by Nancy Tafuri
Published by Greenwillow Books

Arthur's Family Vacation
Written by Marc Brown
Published by Little, Brown & Company

Equipment Estimation

How do two main pieces of baseball equipment measure up with your youngsters? Find out with this simple measurement activity. To prepare, duplicate and cut out three baseball and three bat patterns (page 65). Label each cutout in the ball and bat set with "Too Short," "Just Right," or "Too Long." Then show students a real baseball and bat. Explain to them how each of the two are used in a game of baseball. If desired, pass the ball and bat to each child so that he can hold them; then give each child a 12" length of yarn. Ask him to cut his yarn to the length he believes to be equal to the ball's *circumference*—the distance around the middle of the ball. Then have each child wrap his yarn around the ball to check his estimation. Attach each string to the corresponding baseball cutout. Then follow the same procedure for measuring the length of the bat, giving each child a four-foot length of yarn. Attach these yarn lengths to the appropriately labeled bat cutouts. Compare and discuss the results of each estimation activity.

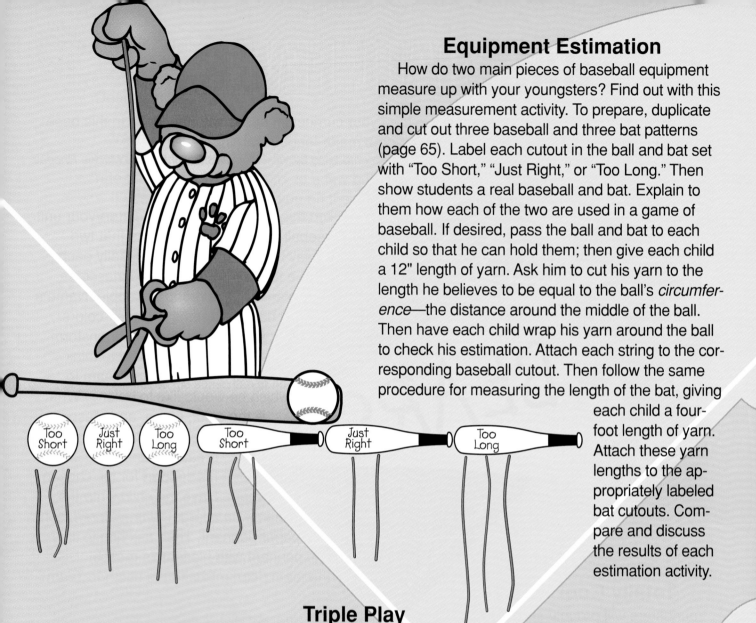

Triple Play

Three cheers for a triple play! Youngsters will be cheering each other on in this adapted version of Concentration. To make the cards, duplicate a supply of the ball, bat, and glove patterns on page 65 on construction paper. Cut out each pattern; then program each set (one ball, one bat, and one glove) with a set of rhyming words or pictures. If desired, laminate the cards for durability.

Tell youngsters that not only do baseball players use a bat and ball, but they also use a special glove while playing the game. Show students a baseball glove, giving each child an opportunity to place it on her hand and to catch a ball in it. Afterward set up the card game by placing all the cards facedown on a table. To play, invite a player to turn over a ball, a bat, and a glove. If all three cards reveal words or pictures from a rhyming set, the child keeps the cards. If the cards do not form a matching set, the child returns them facedown to the table and play continues with the next child. Have each player repeat the procedure, continuing play until all the matches are found. One, two, three…it's a triple play!

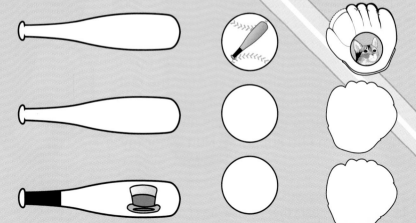

Pick Your Position

Now that youngsters are familiar with the basic baseball equipment, they are most likely eager to use some of it! Before giving students real balls, bats, and gloves, duplicate and cut out a supply of the ball, bat, and glove patterns on page 65 on construction paper. Then describe three of the key player positions in a baseball game—the *pitcher,* the *batter,* and the *catcher.* Tell students that the player in each of these positions uses either a ball, a bat, or a glove. Explain that the pitcher throws the ball to the batter, who uses the bat to hit the ball. If the ball is not hit by the batter, it is caught in the glove of the catcher.

Then invite each child to pick one of the three positions that she would like to play. Write each child's name on a construction-paper cutout corresponding to her chosen position. Attach each cutout to the appropriate column on a three-column graph labeled with the three different baseball positions; then have youngsters discuss the results. Afterward divide your class into groups of three students. Give each student group a baseball, bat, and glove; then invite the students in each group to take turns assuming the positions of pitcher, batter, and catcher. Spring training has begun!

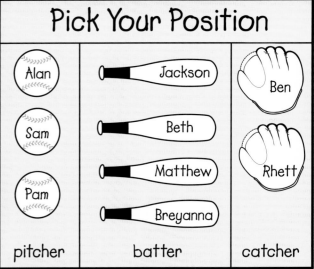

Card Collector's Edition

A baseball player's claim to fame is in the cards—baseball cards, that is! Show a few baseball cards to your class, explaining that the cards give information such as the player's name, his birthdate, his team, his position, and his playing *statistics*—or how well he plays the game. Then invite each child to create his own player's card. To begin, have each child put on his baseball cap (from "Totally Cool Team Caps" on page 61), then strike a pose holding the piece of equipment corresponding to his chosen position in "Pick Your Position." Snap photos of all your players with their gear; then have the pictures developed. Mount each photo on a tagboard card; then write the child's dictated personal and baseball-career information on the card. Ask each student to share his baseball card with the class. Afterward display all the cards with the title "Baseball Hall Of Fame."

Carrie Watts
Born November 4, 1992
All-State Bears
Catcher
100 home runs

Figuring Out The Field

Challenge youngsters to explore the many different shapes found on a baseball field with this idea. First use chalk or long lengths of nylon cording to mark off an outdoor baseball diamond. Then mark a round pitcher's mound and an on-deck circle on the field. Designate rectangular dugout areas just outside of the first and third baselines; then place four square bases around the field. Take your class to the field. Ask one small group at a time to run and stand in any of the areas on the field corresponding to a named shape; then tell youngsters the name for that part of the field—such as *pitcher's mound* or *dugout.* Afterward divide your class into two teams to play a relaxed-rules game of baseball.

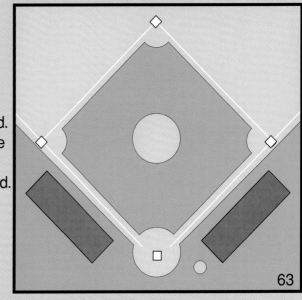

The ABC's Of Baseball

Go into extra innings to give students practice in alphabet recognition. While on the outdoor field (see "Figuring Out The Field" on page 63) or in your classroom, play this no-equipment-needed game of baseball with youngsters. Divide your class into two teams and explain that each team will take a turn at bat. As each team player stands at home plate, "pitch" her a card labeled with a letter of the alphabet. Then ask her to name the letter or a word that begins with that letter sound. If she gives an appropriate response, she has made a hit and advances to first base. If she is unsuccessful, after three attempts, in giving an appropriate response (with helpful coaching from you, of course!), the player is out and returns to her team's bench. Invite each player on the team to take a turn at bat, having each base runner advance around the bases when a hit is made. Continue until the team has scored three runs or made three outs. Then invite the next team to take its turn at bat. Baseball's as easy as ABC.

Take Me Out To The Ball Game!

If you're unable to take your students out to the ball game, try transforming your classroom into a stadium and bring the ball game to students. In advance, videotape a baseball game. Then create a concession stand in your dramatic-play area. Stock the stand with student-prepared packages of peanuts, popcorn, and pretzels. Set up an area for dispensing drinks; then place a cash register and play money in the concession area. In a spacious area in your room, set up a TV and VCR. Position chairs around the TV to resemble stadium seating. Then give each child a paper-slip "ticket" and a few plastic coins for spending. Assign volunteers the roles of concession workers and ticket takers. Invite your little baseball fans into the stadium for the big game. Encourage them to purchase concessions and to sit and watch the game, sharing their observations of the players, the equipment, and the game. Rotate the roles of the students so that each child has the opportunity to be a fan and a stadium worker. Play ball!

Take Me Out To The Library…For A Book About Baseball!

Here's a grand slam selection of books about baseball—just for the fun of it!

Albert's Ballgame
Written by Leslie Tryon
Published by Simon & Schuster Books
For Young Readers

Bats About Baseball
Written by Jean Little and Claire Mackay
Published by Viking Children's Books

Nana Hannah's Piano
Written by Barbara Bottner
Published by The Putnam & Grosset Group

Take Me Out To The Ballgame
Original lyrics by Jack Norworth
Published by Four Winds Press

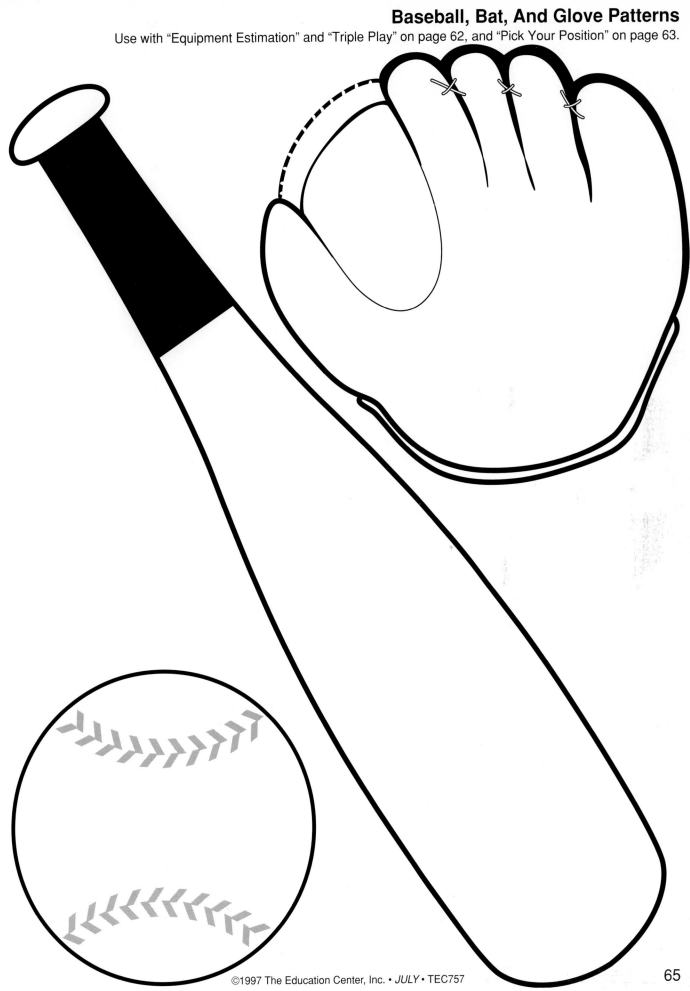

THE SCOOP ON ICE CREAM

Ice cream! Just the mention of this dairy delight evokes screams of excitement from the young and young-at-heart. Use the curriculum-related activities in this unit to give youngsters the scoop on the *whys, hows* and *wows* of ice cream. Yum-yum!

ideas contributed by Suzanne Moore and Mackie Rhodes

A Sweet Surprise

Surprise youngsters with this colorful introduction to your ice-cream unit. To prepare, duplicate and cut from construction paper a spoon pattern (page 72) for each child. Then, just before group time, use a tablecloth to cover a tray holding a container of Neapolitan ice cream and a supply of wide craft sticks. During group time, challenge the class to guess the surprise under the tablecloth, providing descriptive clues as necessary. When youngsters conclude that ice cream is the surprise, remove the cloth to reveal the items on the tray. Then scoop a sample of each different flavor that a child wants to taste onto the end of a separate craft stick. When the tasting is complete, write each child's name on her spoon cutout, then have her attach the cutout to a strip of bulletin-board paper—white, brown, or pink—corresponding to the ice-cream flavor she prefers. Display the paper strips side by side to resemble Neapolitan ice cream; then compare the taste-test results. No matter how you flavor it, ice cream is a favorite!

Cup Or Cone?

While youngsters savor the lingering sweetness from their taste test, tell them about the variety of ways ice cream is prepared and served. Here are a few popular ice-cream fashions to get you started.

- Ice cream in a cup
- Ice-cream cones
- Ice-cream sundaes
- Ice-cream floats
- Banana splits
- Ice-cream pie
- Ice-cream sandwiches
- Ice-cream bars

As a follow-up, invite small groups of students to cut out pictures of different ice-cream treats and dishes from food magazines and grocery-store fliers. Then have each group glue its cutouts onto a large paper scoop. Display the scoops in an ice-cream boat cut from bulletin-board paper. Title the display "In Cups, Cones, Or Dishes, Ice Cream Is 'Yummy-licious'!"

PALATE PLEASERS

Ooooh! All those ice-cream dishes sound so tempting. To satisfy students' dreamy, creamy cravings, set up an ice-cream buffet in your classroom. In advance duplicate a copy of the parent letter on page 72 to send home with each child. After all the items have been brought to class, arrange them in food-bar fashion on a table along with some inspirational pictures of ice-cream dishes. Invite each child to visit the buffet to create, then name, his own ice-cream dream dish. Totally tantalizing!

"I LOVE ICE CREAM!" BOOKLET

Now that youngsters have satisfied their ice-cream-induced cravings, invite them to create these taste-teaser booklets to share with family and friends. For each child make a construction-paper copy of the booklet cover and each booklet page on pages 73–75. Read through the directions for completing each page and gather the necessary materials. For page 3 place an assortment of crayon shavings between sheets of waxed paper. Melt the shavings by ironing over the waxed paper. Instruct each child to cut out her cover and pages, then complete each according to the provided suggestions. Afterward help her sequence and staple her booklet together along the left side.

I Love Ice Cream!

by Antoinette

Ice cream sundaes, 1

Milk shakes, floats, and fruit sorbets, 4

Cover: Write your name. Glue a small photo of yourself (or draw a self-portrait) under your name.

Page 1: Color the dish. Glue construction-paper ice-cream scoops in the dish; then top the scoops with streams of glue tinted to represent chocolate, caramel, strawberry, or pineapple toppings. Sprinkle hole-punched confetti over the glue toppings.

Page 2: Sponge-print the ice-cream pie. Glue thin wisps of cotton onto the top of the pie to represent whipped cream.

Page 3: Cut out ice-cream-scoop shapes from the cooled sheets of waxed paper; then glue the scoops onto the dish.

Page 4: Draw ice-cream scoops in each glass using neon crayons; then paint over the scoops with water-thinned tempera paint.

Page 5: Illustrate your favorite ice-cream dish. Write or dictate a completion to the sentence.

Ice-Cream Making Is A Science

Get your students' minds churning with these activities about the scientific activity that occurs when ice cream is made.

The Main Ingredients

Do your youngsters know what ingredients are used to make ice cream? Or how they are combined to achieve that rich, creamy dessert? Test their ice-cream know-how with this activity. Show students the ingredients for a simple, homemade ice-cream recipe (see "Ice-Cream Machines" on page 69)—milk, ice, sugar, salt, and vanilla flavoring; then explain that these are the main ingredients needed to make ice cream. Ask youngsters to share their ideas on how the ingredients might be combined to make ice cream. Mix a few small batches of ice cream per student directions; then freeze the ice-cream mixtures. Compare the looks, tastes, and textures of the student recipes to a purchased brand of vanilla ice cream. After youngsters conclude that there are certainly differences between the ice creams, explain that ice cream is made in a special way. Then proceed with the activity in "Salt-Free Equals Frost-Free" to begin explaining the complex procedure for making this simple pleasure.

Salt-Free Equals Frost-Free

After taste-testing their ice-cream recipes in "The Main Ingredients," students will most likely realize that the salt doesn't belong *in* the ice-cream mixture! Explain the role of salt in ice-cream making with this activity. Put ten ice cubes in each of two clean, 16-ounce metal cans. Label one of the cans "salt"; then stir seven tablespoons of salt into that can. Leave both cans to sit undisturbed for about five minutes. Afterward invite youngsters to examine the cans and compare their observations. Point out to students that the outside of the ice-filled can has a buildup of water—or *condensation.* But the can containing the ice *and* salt has a frosty exterior. Explain that the salt lowers the temperature of the ice in the can, causing the condensation on the outside of the can to freeze. Then ask youngsters to tell why a container of an ice-cream mixture might be placed inside a salty ice mixture. Guide them to understand that the salty mix creates a colder temperature in which the ice-cream mix can freeze. What a chilling discovery!

ICE-CREAM MACHINES

Transform your students into ice-cream-making machines so they can test their newfound knowledge about the freezing properties of salty ice. To make ice cream, provide each pair of students with a tightly sealed, quart-size zippered plastic bag filled with 1/2 cup of milk, one tablespoon of sugar, and 1/2 teaspoon of vanilla flavoring. Have the pair place the bagged mixture into a gallon-size zippered plastic bag filled with two cups of ice and seven tablespoons of salt. Seal the gallon bag tightly. Wrap the bag in a towel; then ask the partners to take turns shaking the bag. While they work, explain to youngsters that the shaking action will help mix the ingredients and fluff the resulting ice cream to a texture more similar to purchased ice cream. (Remind them of the textural differences observed in "The Main Ingredients" on page 68.) After about five minutes, have the partners remove the small bag from the large one; then scoop out an equal portion of ice cream for each of them to enjoy. The freeze is on!

INSULATION INVESTIGATION

It's meltdown time! Now that youngsters have made their own ice cream, have them explore another property of this frozen favorite—melting! To begin, obtain a regular plastic lunchbox and an insulated lunchbox. Scoop equal portions of ice cream into two separate dishes; then close up each dish of ice cream in one of the lunchboxes. After ten minutes open the boxes, inviting students to compare the two dishes of ice cream. Which is melting faster? Why? Leave the experiment for another ten minutes; then have youngsters once again observe and discuss their findings. If desired set up the experiment at another time, while outdoors. Ask students to share and compare their findings with those from the indoor experiment. Take this opportunity to explain why ice cream melts faster outdoors on a hot day.

Extend this activity with a reading of "Ice Cream," one of the stories in *Frog And Toad All Year* by Arnold Lobel (Scholastic Inc.). Then offer each student a cone of ice cream to eat "lick-ety" split—before it melts!

WE ALL SCREAM FOR ICE CREAM!

Everyone loves ice cream! So why not mix some of these flavorful ice-cream ideas in with your curriculum-related activities and centers? Youngsters will be screaming for more!

SAVE SOME FOR ME!

When youngsters learn this song, they will be equipped with a polite plea to be remembered when the bottom of the ice-cream box is in sight. Simply copy the song on a sheet of chart paper; then sing away!

(sung to the tune of "My Bonnie Lies Over The Ocean")

My mother likes one scoop of ice cream.
My father likes two scoops or three.
My brother likes four scoops with sprinkles.
The whole carton is just right for me!

Chorus:
Please save, please save,
Oh, please save some ice cream for me, for me.
Please save, please save,
Oh, please save some ice cream for me!

My mother likes strawberry ice cream.
My father likes fresh Georgia peach.
My brother likes Swiss chocolate almond.
But I'll take any flavor in reach!

Repeat chorus.

My mother likes milk shakes and malteds.
My father likes fruit nut delight.
My brother likes cherry fudge sundaes.
I just like any ice cream in sight!

Repeat chorus.

Katie
2 scoops
of
chocolate

Will
orange with
sprinkles

A DELICIOUS DISPLAY

Here's a cool display idea and a perfect topping for "Save Some For Me!" Have each child use colored glue to paint a plastic yogurt or margarine container lid to resemble a scoop of ice cream. Invite him to scatter glitter sprinkles or hole-punched nuts and fruit pieces over his ice-cream scoop. After his scoop dries, invite him to mount it onto a construction-paper cone or an ice-cream dish created from a paper-plate half. If desired he might also top his ice cream with a red, milk-jug-lid cherry. Have the child write or dictate a description of his creation. Mount the chart-paper copy of the song on a bulletin board; then surround the song with the completed ice-cream crafts and descriptions. Tempting!

A Triple Scoop Of Center Ideas

Try some of these "scooper-duper" ideas in your classroom centers. Enlarge the cone and scoop patterns (page 72) as desired. Then duplicate, cut out, and program the patterns as indicated for the math and language activities. Place the cutouts in the appropriate centers. As each youngster visits the center, invite him to match each scoop to its corresponding cone. You might also set up the centers suggested in "Other Centers." However you use these ideas in your classroom, the scoop is this—a mound of cool learning opportunities awaits your students!

Math Center

Program each cone with:
- a numeral
- a numeral
- a shape or design
- a time to the hour or half-hour
- a sum from 1 to 10

And its matching scoop with:
- the corresponding number of sprinkles
- the corresponding number word
- an identical shape or design
- a clock face corresponding to the time
- a corresponding addition equation

Language Center

Program each cone with:
- a child's name
- a lowercase letter
- a picture from a rhyming set
- a letter
- a color word

And its matching scoop with:
- a copy of the child's photo
- the corresponding uppercase letter
- the corresponding rhyming picture
- a picture beginning with that letter sound
- the corresponding color

Other Centers

- Stock your dramatic-play center with lots of ice-cream-shop paraphernalia—such as paper-cup cones, foam-ball scoops of ice cream, a variety of plastic dessert dishes, ice-cream scoops, clean (but empty) ice-cream containers, and spoons. Also include notepads, pencils, aprons, tablecloths, play money, and a cash register.

- Put wet sand in your class sand table. Then add ice-cream scoops, plastic dishes, foam cups, and spoons. If desired provide a few water-filled squirt bottles to use as syrup toppings.

Scoop Up A Good Book

The Midnight Eaters
Written by Amy Hest
Published by Four Winds Press

From Milk To Ice Cream
Written by Ali Mitgutsch
Published by Carolrhoda Books, Inc.

Make Mine Ice Cream
Written by Melvin Berger
Published by Newbridge Communications, Inc.

Ice Cream
Written by Stella Keller
Published by Raintree Publishers

Parent Request Letter
Use with "Palate Pleasers" on page 67.

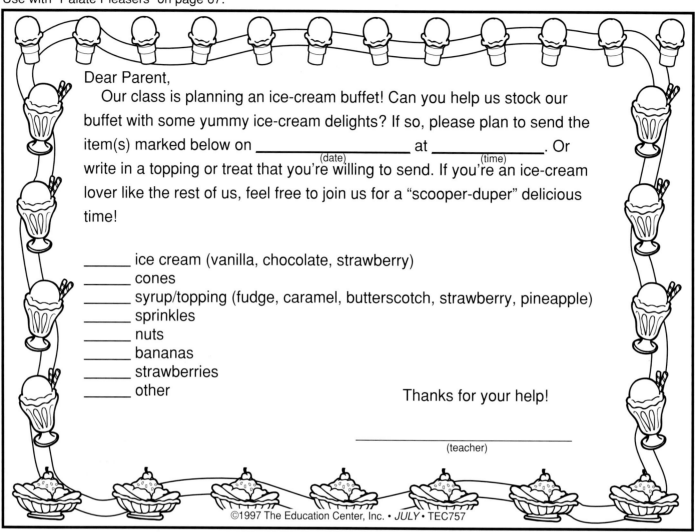

Dear Parent,
    Our class is planning an ice-cream buffet! Can you help us stock our buffet with some yummy ice-cream delights? If so, please plan to send the item(s) marked below on _____ at _____. Or
(date)   (time)
write in a topping or treat that you're willing to send. If you're an ice-cream lover like the rest of us, feel free to join us for a "scooper-duper" delicious time!

_____ ice cream (vanilla, chocolate, strawberry)
_____ cones
_____ syrup/topping (fudge, caramel, butterscotch, strawberry, pineapple)
_____ sprinkles
_____ nuts
_____ bananas
_____ strawberries
_____ other

Thanks for your help!

_____
(teacher)

Cone And Scoop Patterns
Use with "A Triple Scoop Of Center Ideas" on page 71.

Spoon Pattern
Use with "A Sweet Surprise" on page 66.

I Love Ice Cream!

by _____

Ice-cream sundaes,

1

Ice-cream pies,

2

Ice-cream scoops up to the skies!

3

Milk shakes, floats, and fruit sorbets, **4**

I love ice cream lots of ways!

I like _____ best. **5**

Celebrate Recyclables!

Craft a celebration with recyclables! Use the ideas in this unit to make party invitations, favors, decorations, games, and toys.

ideas contributed by Mackie Rhodes and Virginia Zeletzki

The Collection Center

Youngsters will be ready to celebrate their contributions to the recycling effort when they help organize this sorting center. In advance duplicate a copy of the parent letter (page 82) for each child to take home. Then label a box for each type of recyclable item to be brought in by students. Explain to youngsters that a recyclable item is one that can be used in other ways after it has been used for its original purpose. Then name a few recyclable items and examples of additional uses for them. For instance, laundry scoops might be used as sand scoops, or plastic soda bottles might be converted into noisemakers. As each child brings his donations to class, encourage him to sort the items into the appropriate boxes in the recycling center. After your recyclable collection has grown to an adequate proportion, invite youngsters to use the items to prepare the party crafts and projects in this unit.

A Special Invitation

These sparkly, pressed-pulp invitations are perfect for communicating the objective of your class celebration—recycling! To begin, duplicate the heart pattern on page 83 onto several sheets of tagboard; then cut out each pattern to serve as a large heart template. Then program the smaller heart invitation and duplicate a copy for each child onto copy paper.

Divide your class into small groups of students. Working with one group at a time, ask the students to tear newspaper into small pieces and put the pieces into a container of water. After the paper softens, transfer it to a blender. Add a sprinkling of glitter; then cover the mixture with water. Blend the mixture into a pulp with the consistency of thin oatmeal. (Add water as necessary to allow the blade to turn easily through the mixture.) Then invite each child to squeeze a handful of the watery pulp into a ball. Have her flatten her ball into a patty on a smooth tray, then cover the patty with a sheet of plastic canvas. Help the child angle her tray over a sink or dishpan, then press along the canvas to squeeze the excess water from her patty. Set the pressed pulp patty—now a wet sheet of recycled paper—aside to dry.

After the paper dries, invite each child to trace the large heart template onto her paper, then cut along the resulting outline. Have her cut out and glue the invitation heart cutout to one side of her pulp-paper heart, then decorate the other side with markers or other craft items. Encourage each child to take the invitation home to her family.

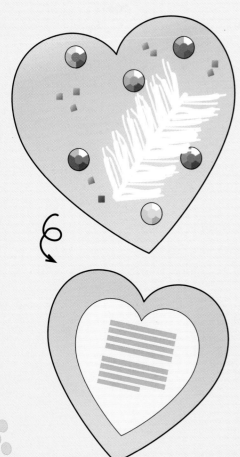

76

A Flowery Favor

Now that the invitations have been sent, have youngsters create these neat candy holders for their class celebration. To prepare, gather a class supply of spray-can lids. Enlarge the flower pattern on page 84 so that the circle size approximates the size of the plastic lids to be used; then duplicate a class supply of the pattern on construction paper. Help each child cut out a flower pattern, and then cut along the dotted lines inside the circle. Fit each cutout over a lid, hot-gluing the cut sections to the inside of the lid so that it resembles a flower. After the glue sets, tuck a tissue-paper lining into the lid. Fill the resulting flower cup with the candy of your choice. Blooming good!

Party Toppers

Convert a plain, black-and-white section of newspaper into a fashionable party hat with this idea. To begin, cover two or three sheets of newspaper with berry-basket or egg-carton paint prints. After the paint dries, position the sheets over a head-size bowl so that the paper corners do not overlap (see illustration). Shape the paper snugly over the bowl, taping it as necessary so that it retains the shape when the bowl is removed. Roll the rim of the resulting hat to the desired width. Or, for a really unique look, leave the hat rim as it is. If desired, hot-glue a ribbon or some feathers onto the hat. Then, during the celebration, invite students to wear their recycled hats. These hats are tops!

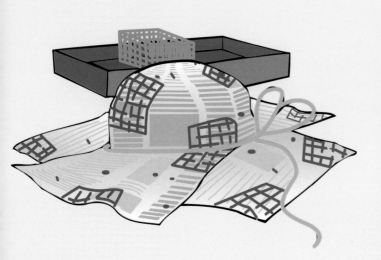

Gifts For Guests

Surprise your party guests with these adorable flower-cart gifts. To make one, hot-glue milk-jug-lid wheels to opposite sides of a plastic laundry scoop. Fit a block of Styrofoam® into the resulting cart; then insert several stems of small artificial flowers into the foam block. Invite each child to present a flower cart to a party guest as a reminder to recycle and reuse those throw-away items.

77

Dandy Displays

Here are some dandy ideas for making decorative display pieces from recyclable items.

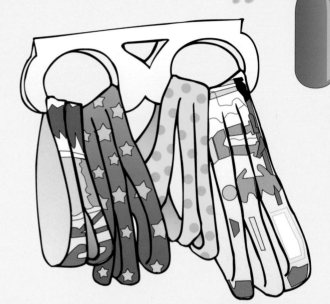

Party Streamers

Here's a colorful use for those plastic six-pack rings and old comics or used gift wrap. Have each child cut long strips from newspaper comics or gift-wrap paper. Instruct her to thread each paper strip through a loop of a plastic six-pack ring, then glue the ends of each strip together. If desired, invite her to cut each strip into several more narrow strips, being careful not to cut through the plastic ring. Hang the resulting party streamers in the doorway, around the windows, or from the ceiling to create a "Celebrate Recyclables!" atmosphere.

Pencil-Poked Pooches

Have pencil, will poke—especially when a meat tray is involved! Give youngsters a good reason to poke holes in a meat tray with this idea. Duplicate the dog pattern on page 84 onto tagboard. Cut out the pattern to use as a template. To make a pencil-poked pooch, trace the template onto a meat tray using a permanent marker; then use a pencil to poke holes inside the resulting outline. Glue a colored construction-paper backing to the tray. Then, if desired, use craft items to create a mouth, ears, and eyes for the dog. Display these creative canines during your recyclables party. Here, poochy, poochy!

Meat-Tray Masterpieces

Draw out the artistic flair in your students with this print-block activity. For each child, cut away the sides of a foam meat tray so that only the flat bottom remains. Give each child a blunt-point pencil and a meat-tray bottom. Ask the child to etch a design or picture on the foam tray; then have him paint the etched side of the tray with a mixture of tempera paint and a small amount of dishwashing liquid. Have him press the painted side of the tray onto a sheet of newspaper or the back of a piece of recycled gift-wrap paper. Help the child carefully lift the tray off the paper, leaving an imprint of his etched drawing. After the paint dries, draw a two-inch border around the child's painting; then have him cut out his picture along the lines and discard the extra paper. To frame his painting, have the child fold over, then glue down, each side of his paper . Display the creations with the title "Meat-Tray Masterpieces."

Party Games

No party is complete without games. Make these games from recyclables; then recycle the fun each time youngsters play them.

Listen 'n' Look

Pass out the cards and start the game—and the learning! This card game will promote picture identification and listening skills. To make the cards, cut off the fronts of a supply of old greeting cards; then make a list of the variety of things pictured on the card fronts. Laminate the list for repeated use. Then, playing with one small group of students at a time, pass an equal number of cards to each child in the group. Set the remaining cards aside. To play, call out a word from your list, marking it with a wipe-off marker. If a child has a card picturing the named item, he places it faceup on the table and points out the item. Continue the game until each child has discarded all his cards in this manner. Then collect and shuffle the cards, wipe off your word list, and prepare the next group for a round of play.

Word List
Santa Claus
cow
dinosaur
dog
house
fence

Cereal Box "Marbles"

This modified game of marbles requires a good eye and accurate aim. Create a cereal-box marble alley by cutting several arched openings in the box as shown. Support the box against a wall; then invite a child to roll soda-bottle caps, toilet-paper-tube rings, or foil balls into the box openings. If desired, label each opening with a numeral; then challenge the child to name which opening he will try to hit each time he rolls an item. Ready…aim…roll!

Recyclables Ring Toss

Target some eye-hand coordination practice with this ring toss game. To prepare the game, cut apart the loops from a six-pack soda-bottle ring, trimming away any excess plastic so that nicely formed, individual rings are created. If desired, color each ring with a permanent marker so that it is more visible. Make a target from a plastic soda bottle by partially filling it with sand, then replacing the lid. Or poke the handles of several plastic spoons into a foam block to form posts. Invite each child, in turn, to toss the rings at the target. Three rings on the target! Wow!

Toy Time

No need to run out and buy toy favors for the party! Simply make these fun and fascinating goodies from your collection of recyclables.

Soda-Bottle Sweeties

These soda-bottle dolls will offer just the invitation needed to keep youngsters returning to the housekeeping or block center. To make a doll, remove the label from a plastic soda bottle; then partially fill the bottle with sand. Hot-glue the lid onto the bottle. Paint torn pieces of newspaper with water-thinned glue; then cover the bottle with the newspaper. After the paper dries, paint the bottle to resemble clothing on a doll's body. Allow the paint to dry; then hot-glue plastic spoon arms to the bottle-body. Use one-half of a toilet-paper tube to represent the head. Draw a face on the tube, or use craft items to create a face; then glue on newspaper-strip hair. Complete the doll by positioning, then hot-gluing, the tube-head over the bottle top. Put the dolls in one or more centers for party-time play; then invite each child to take his doll home after the celebration. So sweet!

S-S-S-Surprise!

Give youngsters an opportunity to spring some humor on their unsuspecting party guests with this silly snake puppet. To make a puppet, hot-glue wiggle eyes onto the back of a plastic spoon; then hot-glue a pull strip from a milk-jug lid onto the tip of the spoon to represent a snake's tongue. Color a Styrofoam® cup to resemble a log. Gently push the handle of the snake spoon through the bottom of the cup. To make the snake "slither" in and out of the log, simply slide the spoon in and out through the cup. Teach youngsters the rhyme below, directing them to keep one hand over the open end of their logs until the last line. At this time, they will make their surprise snakes crawl out of their logs. After surprising their party guests, encourage each child to surprise his family and friends at home with his snake puppet.

He wiggles and wiggles, slides and slides.
Inside my log this creature hides.
A long, quick tongue,
And two round eyes.
Come out, my little snake surprise!
S-s-s-s-s-s!

Catch-A-Cap

This challenging toy will fascinate youngsters and test their "stick-to-itiveness." To make a catch-a-cap, poke about one-third of a wide craft stick through the bottom of a Styrofoam® cup so that the stick slides against the cup wall. Hot-glue the stick to the cup wall, being careful not to melt a hole in the cup. Punch a hole in the opposite top rim of the cup. Thread the end of a 12-inch length of yarn through the hole and tie it in place. Then hot-glue the other end of the yarn to the inside of a plastic soda cap or milk-jug lid. To use the toy, hold it by the stick handle and swing it forward and upward, attempting to catch the lid in the cup. Keep trying…you know you can do it!

Nifty Nesters

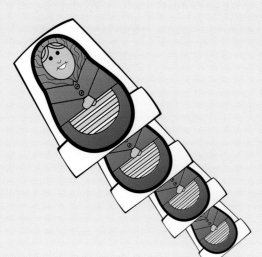

When youngsters play with these nesting dolls, they'll get plenty of practice in size seriation and pretend play. To make a set of dolls, duplicate the doll patterns (page 85) on construction paper. Color each pattern; then cut out the patterns along the bold lines. Glue each cutout onto an inverted cup corresponding to the size of the doll cutout. Have each student make his own set of dolls in this manner. Then, during your class celebration, promote play with the doll sets by placing them in several centers. After the party, send each child's doll set home with him.

Zoom, Zoom, Va-room!

Prepare to witness some high-speed dramatic play when youngsters create different vehicles from assorted boxes. Invite each child to select a box from the recycling center; then ask her to create a vehicle—such as a car, train, or plane—using the box, plastic lids, and other recyclable items. Assist each child as necessary to hot-glue items to her creation. Then ask her to describe her vehicle to the class. Collect the vehicles and put them aside until the day of your celebration.

Remember…

Recyclables can be used at any time for a multitude of purposes. Please keep your class in the habit of recycling and reusing items for class activities and special events. Celebrate recyclables year-round!

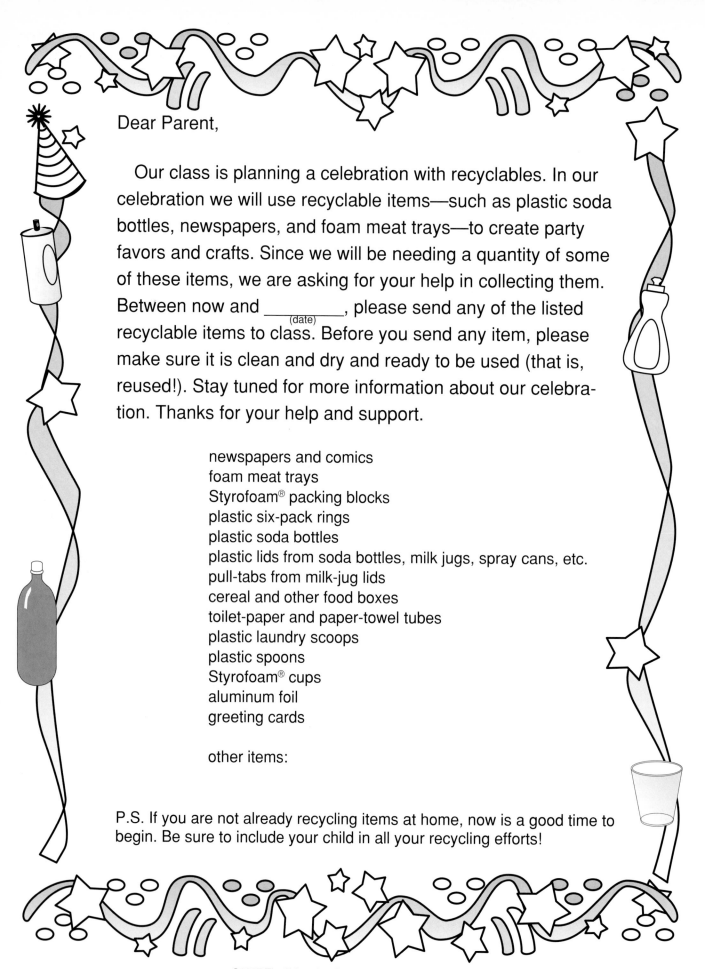

Dear Parent,

Our class is planning a celebration with recyclables. In our celebration we will use recyclable items—such as plastic soda bottles, newspapers, and foam meat trays—to create party favors and crafts. Since we will be needing a quantity of some of these items, we are asking for your help in collecting them. Between now and _____, please send any of the listed
(date)
recyclable items to class. Before you send any item, please make sure it is clean and dry and ready to be used (that is, reused!). Stay tuned for more information about our celebration. Thanks for your help and support.

newspapers and comics
foam meat trays
Styrofoam® packing blocks
plastic six-pack rings
plastic soda bottles
plastic lids from soda bottles, milk jugs, spray cans, etc.
pull-tabs from milk-jug lids
cereal and other food boxes
toilet-paper and paper-towel tubes
plastic laundry scoops
plastic spoons
Styrofoam® cups
aluminum foil
greeting cards

other items:

P.S. If you are not already recycling items at home, now is a good time to begin. Be sure to include your child in all your recycling efforts!

Note To The Teacher: Use with "The Collection Center" on page 76.

Cereal boxes, comics, and papery things.
Meat trays, bottles, and plastic soda rings.
Such dandy creations from our imaginings.
Come help celebrate our recyclings!

Please join us to celebrate all the useful and
fun crafts, toys, and games we've created
from recyclables on _____ at
                          (date)

_____.
   (time)

©1997 The Education Center, Inc.

Flower Pattern
Use with "A Flowery Favor" on page 77.

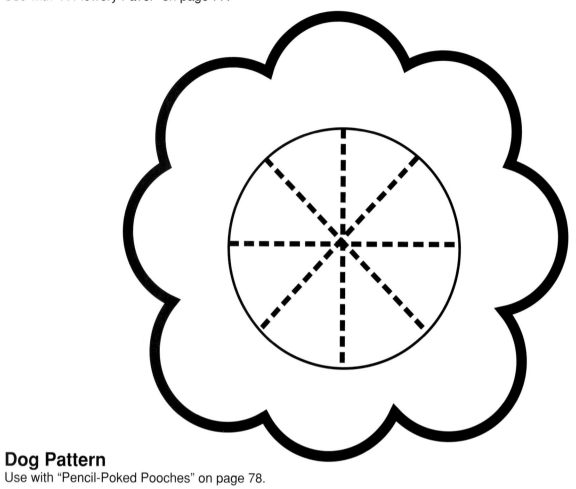

Dog Pattern
Use with "Pencil-Poked Pooches" on page 78.

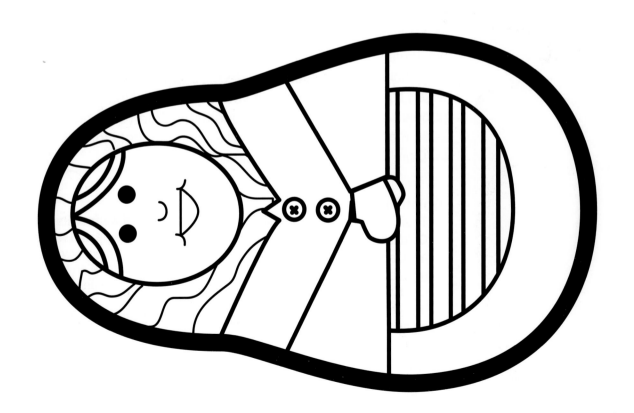

My Aquarium

Little ones will put their aquarium know-how to good use when making these booklets. Reproduce a class supply of the booklet cover and pages on pages 92–94 onto white construction paper; then cut them apart. Read through the directions below for completing each booklet page; then gather the necessary art supplies. Have each student complete a set of pages. When each youngster's pages are complete, instruct him to sequence the pages; then staple his booklet together along the left side. Finally, glue the child's picture onto the diver's helmet on page 5 of his booklet.

Cover: Color as desired.
Page 1: Glue aquarium gravel within the bag outline.
Page 2: Glue torn, green tissue-paper strips onto the page to resemble plants.
Page 3: Color the bucket blue to resemble water.
Page 4: Color the fish.
Page 5: Color the scene with crayons; then paint over it with diluted blue paint.

Fish Food

Continue your aquarium activities by having each child make his own edible aquarium. To make one, spread soft cream cheese that has been tinted with blue food coloring onto a large rectangular cracker. Crumble a few pretzel sticks; then arrange them along the bottom of the cracker to resemble gravel. Next place slivered celery sticks atop the cracker to resemble plants. Count out several fish-shaped crackers; then place them on the cream cheese. Glub, glub, good!

Goldfish Math

If your little ones like those edible aquariums, invite them to nibble on some more fish crackers after this fishbowl math activity. Reproduce a class supply of the sorting sheet on page 96. Provide each child with a sorting sheet to color and a resealable plastic bag containing varying amounts of three flavors of goldfish crackers. Invite a child to predict how many fish are in his bag. Then have him sort the fish—according to flavor—atop the circles on his sorting sheet. Encourage him to count each type of fish, then compare the amounts. Then invite him to eat his manipulatives. One nibble and he'll be hooked!

There Are Other Fish In The Sea

Now that youngsters know about goldfish and guppies, they'll be excited to learn about other fish that live in aquariums, ponds, rivers, lakes—and the sea! Share these common attributes of fish; then use the follow-up activities for some fishy fun!

How Does A Fish Eat?
A fish gathers food in a variety of ways depending on where it lives and the shape of its mouth.
- A fish with an upturned mouth eats insects from the water's surface.
- A fish with a mouth that faces forward can feed anywhere.
- A bottom-feeding fish has a mouth that is downturned, allowing it to vacuum food from below.

How Does A Fish Breathe?
A fish receives oxygen by taking in water through its mouth. Oxygen is removed as the water passes over the gills.

How Does A Fish Swim?
- A fish has a streamlined body and pointed head that move easily through the water.
- Powerful muscles in the body and tail help a fish push its way through water.
- A fish's fins help it turn and stay balanced in the water.

Swimmy Similarites

Use this poem to teach your little fisher folk some striking fish similarities.

Fish come in many shapes and sizes,
And in different colors, too!
Some fish are red; some fish are yellow;
And some are even blue.

But fishes' bodies are quite alike;
This fact cannot go unsaid.
Every fish has a tail and some fins,
And—of course—a head.

A fish's fins can help it to turn,
And to keep it on its course.
A fish's tail goes from side to side;
It pushes with great force.

A fish is covered with many scales.
The scales protect the skin
From parasites, rocks, and enemies
That bite with toothy grins!

A fish takes water into its mouth,
And over the gills it goes.
The gills take air for the fish to breathe
As the fish swims to and fro.

Fishy Art

Invite students to create schools of fanciful fish when visiting these fun art centers. Have each child select one fish for later use when illustrating a class book (see "In Our Aquarium I See…"); then display the remainder of the fish in your classroom.

Sponge-Painted Fish

Stock this center with several fish-shaped sponges, tempera paint, and shallow paint trays. To make a fish, a child dips a sponge into tempera paint, and then presses it onto a sheet of construction paper. When the paint is dry, he glues a wiggle eye onto the fish, then cuts it out.

Paper-Plate Fish

Stock a center with paper-plate fish (see illustration), wiggle eyes, glue, scissors, and a variety of craft supplies—such as construction-paper scraps, rickrack, foil, sequins, buttons, and fabric scraps. A child may embellish a fish using his choice of craft materials.

Crayon-Resist Fish

Stock this center with neon crayons, white construction paper, and diluted blue paint. Have a child use the crayons to draw fish on a sheet of white construction paper. Then have her brush the drawing with diluted blue paint. When the paint is dry, instruct her to cut out the fish.

Rainbow Fish

Stock this center with a supply of paper-plate fish (see illustration), colored tissue-paper squares, thinned glue, and brushes. Have a child brush thinned glue over a fish, then press tissue squares onto the glue. To complete his fish, have him glue on a wiggle eye.

In Our Aquarium I See…

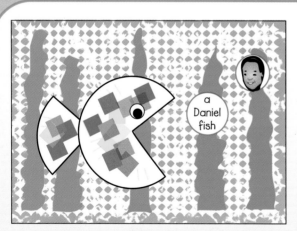

The ancient Greeks believed everything on land had a counterpart underwater. It's easy to believe that when we consider the names of some fish, such as *catfish, dogfish,* and *butterfly fish.* Delight your little ones by suggesting that they create a class book in which fish will be named after themselves!

To prepare a page, have a child paint a sheet of bubble wrap with blue and green paint, then press the bubble wrap onto a large sheet of construction paper to make a print. When the paint is dry, have her select one of her previously made fish (see "Fishy Art") to attach to the print. Next have her cut out construction-paper strips to resemble aquatic plants, then glue them to the print. To complete the child's page, personalize a white construction-paper circle as shown. Glue a color copy of the child's picture to a second white paper circle. Add the circles to the print to represent bubbles. Bind the pages together; then title the book, "In Our Aquarium I See…." Place the book in your aquarium center for all your little fish to enjoy.

Fish-A-Doodle

Teach your young artists to draw fish with this nifty poem. Write the poem and illustrate each step on a sheet of chart paper. Demonstrate the steps as you read the poem aloud. Place the chart in your aquarium center along with paper, crayons, markers, scissors, and glue. Invite a child to refer to the chart to draw more fish. Encourage youngsters to add other fish body parts—such as fins or gills—to their drawings before cutting out the fish and gluing them around the poem.

Draw A Fish

First draw an *X*—big or small;
Small for a little fish, or big for a tall.

The fish's body shows up next.
Draw half an oval; connect it to the *X*.

Make the tail with a straight, straight line.
Close up the *X* for a fish that's mighty fine!

Cinn-A-Fish

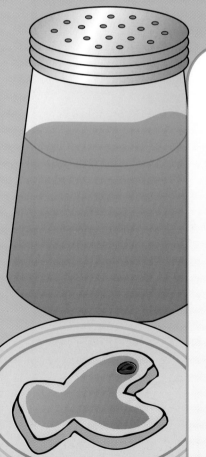

What's better than drawing fish? Eating them, of course! Especially these tasty treats! First duplicate page 96 for later use. Then remove page 95 and glue it to a sheet of tagboard. Cut apart the cards; then laminate them for durability, if desired. Arrange the ingredients, utensils, and supplies along with the recipe cards at a table. Then invite each child to prepare a Cinn-A-Fish. Mmmm, good!

Cinn-A-Fish

Ingredients For One:
1 refrigerated biscuit
1 raisin
cinnamon-sugar mixture

Utensils And Supplies:
1 plastic knife per child
1 paper plate per child
empty shaker
aluminum foil
toaster oven
permanent marker

Teacher Preparation:
Place the cinnamon-sugar mixture in a clean shaker. For each child, use a permanent marker to personalize a foil square. Place one refrigerated biscuit on each foil square. Preheat the toaster oven to the temperature recommended on the biscuit package. Closely supervise the baking process and bake the Cinn-A-Fish following the biscuit package directions.

My Aquarium

by _____

water

gravel

The gravel.

1

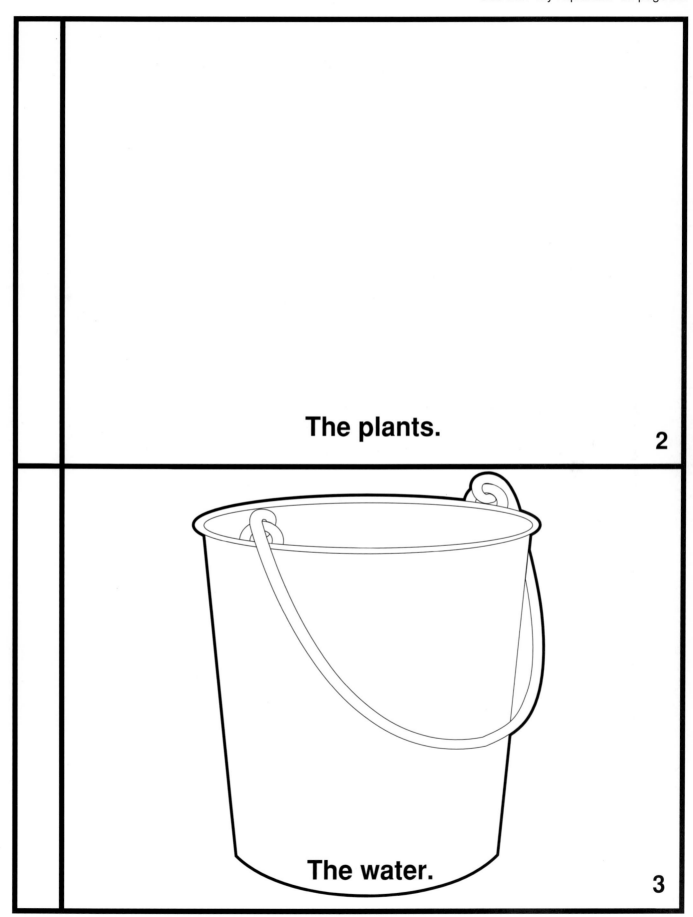

The plants.

2

The water.

3

The fish.

4

My aquarium!

5